The Resilient Family Farm

Supporting Agricultural Development and Rural Economic Growth

Gaye Burpee and Kim Wilson

ITDG
PUBLISHING

Published by ITDG Publishing
The Schumacher Centre for Technology and Development
Bourton Hall, Bourton-on-Dunsmore, Rugby, Warwickshire CV23 9QZ, UK
www.itdgpublishing.org.uk

© Catholic Relief Services 2004

First published in 2004

ISBN 1 85339 592 7

A catalogue record for this book is available from the British Library.

ITDG Publishing is the publishing arm of the Intermediate Technology
Development Group. Our mission is to build the skills and capacity of people
in developing countries through the dissemination of information in all forms,
enabling them to improve the quality of their lives and that of future generations.

Drawings by Kim Wilson
Photographs by Gaye Burpee
Graphic design by Jim Doyle
Printed in Great Britain by Antony Rowe Limited, Wiltshire

Contents

Acknowledgements

The Resilient Family Farm draws on the authors' experiences and research in international development, working with and learning from the wisdom, pluck and innovation of farmers and villagers from Africa, Asia, Latin America and the Caribbean. In the midst of demanding schedules, colleagues from around the world contributed thoughtful, careful and sometimes extensive review comments for which we are most grateful – Jill Donahue (Southern Africa), Kamal Bhattacharyaa (India), Polly Ericksen (CRS headquarters), Jenny Aker (West Africa), Kristen Sample (Latin America), David Leege (Rwanda), Numa Shams (Cambodia), Jim Hudock (Southeast Asia) and Patrick McAllister (headquarters).

The authors also gratefully acknowledge the support provided by the office of Food for Peace (DCHA/FFP), USAID, under the terms of Award Number FAO-A-00-98-00046-00. The views expressed in this publication are those of the authors and do not necessarily represent the views of Catholic Relief Services or the US Agency for International Development.

Introduction

The story

Lin rises at 5:00 a.m. before the roosters begin crowing. She walks two miles to the edge of the forest to collect wood for fuel and returns home to cook breakfast for her family. This begins her day of harvesting rice, looking after her children, thatching part of her roof with rice straw, tending poultry and doing laundry.

Vietnam

Lin's husband rises early as well. Harvest is always demanding, and he works in the fields all day. Lin is glad he has returned. Three months ago, he left to take a job as a day laborer some 100 kilometers away. While he was gone, there was much to be done on the farm and Lin had no help, save her small children. Food was scarce so they ate little and conserved their energy by sleeping whenever they could. Lin wrapped cloth firmly around the children's bellies, so they would not cry from hunger. Her neighbor brought a tea made from leaves that stop the stomach from hurting.

Lin's story is about many families in many countries. Where farm families used to endure a hunger season of one month each year right before harvest, now they endure two, three, four, five, even six months of hunger. As trees vanish and topsoils are depleted in many areas farmed by the poorest, as weather becomes more variable and groundwater disappears, it becomes harder for crops to withstand drought, floods, weeds, pests and disease, and it becomes harder for farmers to feed their families.[1,2] Farms in Lin's watershed are able to

[1] Worldwatch Institute, *Vital Signs 2001* (New York, NY: W.W. Norton & Company, 2001), 12, 17–19, 32.

[2] Worldwatch Institute, *State of the World 2001* (New York, NY: W.W. Norton & Company, 2001), 46, 52–53.

produce less and less. Families split up as husbands try to find what little work there is far away. Like Lin, many wives are left to run the farm alone.

Some farm families, though, are able to weather the stresses brought on by the natural and social world. These families spend their days mending fish ponds and goat pens, bringing chicken manure to the compost heap, collecting eggs to sell to neighbors, picking vegetables to preserve, turning nitrogen-fixing plants back into the soil as fertilizer, pruning the low branches of hardwood trees for firewood, gathering low-hanging fruit to eat and feeding home-grown maize to a pig. They devote time to finding better ways to control insects, learning about a neighbor's weed-control method, testing new varieties of seed and recharging their subsurface aquifers through carefully designed, yet simple, irrigation systems.

These families have found a fruitful mix of life-giving activities that sustain their tiny farms throughout the hunger season. Their resilient farms blend a variety of income-generating activities with low-cost organic fertilizers and farm-produced pest controls. They work the same size plots of land as their poorer neighbors, yet are able to produce one-third more year after year. Social scientists would call these farm families 'positive deviants'. What is their secret?

The task of the farm family

Small family farms constitute much of the world's tropical agriculture in the many countries still depending on agriculture for economic growth. In rural areas, smallholder farms employ the vast majority of adults and youths and generate most of the income produced. These farms are the patches of land that dot rural landscapes, quilting together the smallest fields, orchards, gardens, fish ponds and pastures into life-giving resources for the poorest families.

While such farms may be small, by no means are they simple.[1] Family farms the world over consist of a fine web of social, economic, environmental and communal activities. However, the *healthy* family farm

---

[1] Chen, Martha Alter and Elizabeth Dunn, *Household Economic Portfolios* (Washington, DC: US Agency for International Development. USAID AIMS project, AIMS Brief Number 3, 1996). See 'Desk Studies' under 'AIMS publications' at www.mip.org.

is not only diverse, but also efficient and generally much better able to stave off threats, yield a livelihood for the farming family and provide for the livelihoods of future families.

Everything grown on the family farm has many uses. The secret of the healthy family farm is that it taps into and takes full advantage of the diversity. Rice paddies yield not only rice to eat, but can also yield fish to dry and sell, straw to compost and grain alcohol to drink. Millet

Gambia

fields produce grain, but also fodder and beer. Garlic flavors meals, reduces cholesterol and enhances immune systems. But when mixed with water and applied to plants, garlic can also ward off garden pests. Many legume species can be consumed as animal fodder or beans, but they can also be turned into the soil as 'green manure' for a later, more profitable crop.

Dozens of activities can spring up around primary crops and animals. Silk is spun, cream becomes butter. Fruits are dried, ground nuts roasted, seeds pressed into oil, leaves crushed into tea. Rice straw is transformed into livestock feed, duck cages and floor mats; chili pepper becomes chutney or pesticide; thick vetiver grass mutes the wind, holds the soil and even becomes perfume.

Above all, the family farm is important because it is made up of people – mothers, fathers, grandparents, children and grandchildren. Family labor provides the small farm with one of its greatest resources and its main comparative advantage over larger commercial farms. Small family farms are also the cornerstone of an important way of life in rural areas and the guardian of rich cultural traditions.

But to work the farm and improve their lives, members of farm families need nutritious foods, clean water, good healthcare, training, schooling, the opportunity to expand and improve their farming enterprise and the freedom to enjoy communal and family activities. Taken together, this is a tall order.

A resilient farm

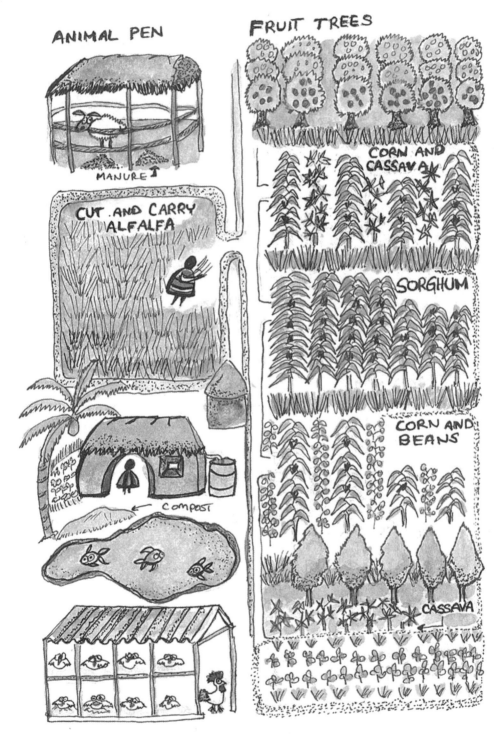

ANIMAL PEN

FRUIT TREES

MANURE

CUT AND CARRY ALFALFA

CORN AND CASSAVA

SORGHUM

CORN AND BEANS

COMPOST

CASSAVA

A resilient farm

This example of a resilient farm combines grain and vegetable production for subsistence with income-generating fruit and micro-livestock production. The location of the nitrogen-rich alfalfa field is rotated annually with the grain crops to continually enrich the soil. Animal manure and compost additions also enrich the soil and improve drainage.

Vetiver grass, which grows along the contour of the slope, serves as a 'live barrier', preventing soil erosion and water runoff. Generally crops are planted in rows parallel to the live barrier, but this year the farm family is planting grains in rows perpendicular to the horizontal contour line. They want to see if it helps crop roots withstand the waterlogging that occurs in their heavy clay soils several times a year, when sporadic rain is especially heavy between longer drought spells.

The animals are penned for easier management and disease control. The house rooftop supports a water harvesting system that provides clean rainwater for domestic use and better health. Fish provide year-round protein. The bottom of the pond is dredged manually to keep it deep enough to withstand lower water levels in the dry season. Rich silt from the bottom is added to the vegetable garden and crop fields.

For the farm to survive and prosper, the family must find the right balance between those activities that use up and those that replenish the farm's natural capital – those resources that will continue to serve the farm in years to come. When these activities are appropriately balanced, the farm approaches our ideal of a *high-return conservation farm*, or what we are calling in this book a *resilient farm*. These resilient farms are managed by families who are more successful at producing, earning, weathering and adapting to change than their neighbors. They are the positive deviants. Their success serves as a model and beginning.

Supporting the family farm

Time was when many small family farms in the tropics sustained themselves in peace. The farm was a family effort with each member pitching in to keep the farm humming. It was a communal effort with neighbor helping neighbor. While the family farm was not without problems and rarely grew wealthy, it was able to provide for its members.

Enter global warming and its more hostile climate patterns. Enter war and its devastation of entire landscapes. Enter the Green Revolution, with its beneficial inputs and technologies geared to larger farms and its small farm advice aimed at single-crop cultivation. Enter increasing rural populations with their competing demands for farmland – building towns, houses and roads; felling trees for lumber, fuel and home sites; driving small family farms to the very margins of cultivated land. Enter this century where international forces of supply and demand influence even the most rural economies.

These increasing stresses on small family farms are calling us, members of the development community, to re-examine ways of supporting rural people and their environments. How can we limit the potential harm of geo-political forces and at the same time plug the farm family into the resources of a global marketplace? How can we balance local stresses within individual watersheds with the demands of an international economy? How can we cope with more erratic weather patterns? How can we simultaneously address the problems and immediacy of farm life with the scope and power of an information world?

Indonesia

6

These are a few of the questions facing development organizations today. Increasing stress triggers increasing change and challenges us to work with farm families in more innovative ways. Responding to these questions and the questions we do not yet know to ask requires us to develop agile programs effective in a world of constant change.

About the book

The Resilient Family Farm is not intended as a technical guide. It is a primer for those who contribute – or plan to contribute – to rural development. It is for donors who would like to understand better the challenges of farm life. It is for practitioners in all development sectors whose work in some way touches on the smallest farm families. It is for newcomers to development who know nothing about small-scale farming. It is for seasoned practitioners and advisers who may understand their own work in agriculture, health or microfinance, but are not as familiar with the work of other sectors as it applies to the family farm. Finally, it is for anyone who knows or has come to understand that the complexity of the smallest farms demands complete, rather than partial, responses and that complete responses require an appreciation of the rich interconnectedness of farm life.

The book focuses on development organizations – local and international organizations that support rural economies in the developing world. These organizations – mostly with a focus on agriculture and conservation, microfinance, health, education, construction and engineering – have seen success, but also an unnecessary measure of failure. The authors believe that a deeper understanding of the family farm, coupled with insights into the agricultural and financial services sectors of development, will increase success and prevent harmful impacts of projects on the farm family, their communities and their watersheds.

The conclusions throughout the text and the recommendations in the sections titled 'Some cardinal rules' are

7

based on the experiences of the authors. *The Resilient Family Farm* is not meant to be a scholarly treatise, based on thorough data collection, careful replication and statistically significant analyses. Rather, it has been written as a vehicle to share with others our field observations and lessons, to clarify for readers the challenges and realities of those we serve and to present our best thinking about ways to improve support to small farm families. For these reasons, the use of citations in the text is minimal. Suggestions for further reading are found in the Resources section.

Throughout the text there are short, boxed examples of development success and failure. These examples are drawn from the experiences of the authors and their colleagues in the international relief and development community. Names of organizations have been omitted to avoid unproductive negative attention to well-meaning private, voluntary and non-governmental organizations, while the experiences described underscore the clear need for change.

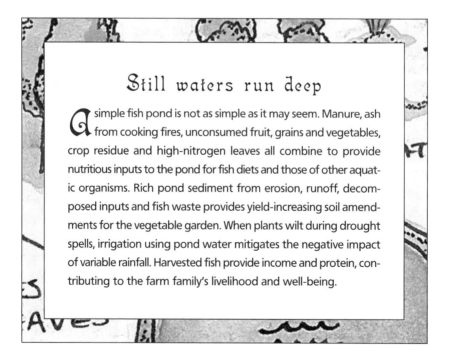

Still waters run deep

A simple fish pond is not as simple as it may seem. Manure, ash from cooking fires, unconsumed fruit, grains and vegetables, crop residue and high-nitrogen leaves all combine to provide nutritious inputs to the pond for fish diets and those of other aquatic organisms. Rich pond sediment from erosion, runoff, decomposed inputs and fish waste provides yield-increasing soil amendments for the vegetable garden. When plants wilt during drought spells, irrigation using pond water mitigates the negative impact of variable rainfall. Harvested fish provide income and protein, contributing to the farm family's livelihood and well-being.

Still waters run deep

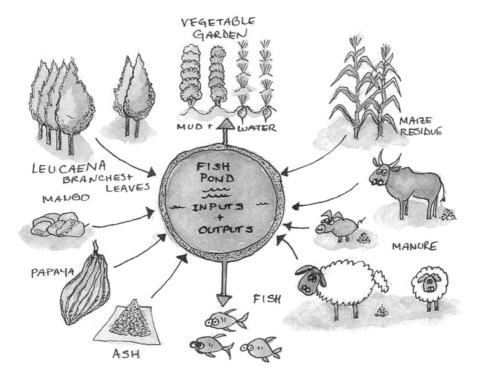

The four chapters of Part I highlight the economic and ecological realities of the small family farm as follows:

Chapter 1: Farm families and their social environment explains who farm families are, what their multiple roles and responsibilities are, why they and their ways of life are worth serving and saving, and how their social, economic and political environment both limits and supports them.

Chapter 2: Farm families and their natural environment reviews the influences of natural forces on the farm and the benefits of natural resources to the small farm family, exploring ways in which families can and do manage these forces and resources to the farm's permanent advantage.

Chapter 3: The family farm as an agricultural system shows how careful stewardship and wise management of closely related farming activities results in many synergies that serve to limit waste, maximize production and replenish resources for future farming activities.

Chapter 4: The family farm as an economic system explains the multiple businesses that constitute the smallest family farms. This chapter reviews the relationship between the farm's many income-generating activities and the economic elements that contribute to their success.

The eight chapters of Part II examine the role of development organizations in supporting farm families who cope with these realities and offer key insights for practitioners in all development sectors. These chapters are as follows:

Chapter 5: Resilient farming reviews the methods used to strengthen farming during the Green Revolution in the 1960s and 1970s and their shortcomings for the poorest farm families. It proposes a general approach that combines the best of traditional farming with modern breakthroughs in agriculture.

Chapter 6: The ripple effect addresses agricultural extension – the work of supporting small farm agriculture through on-farm training and technical support. It focuses on sustainable agriculture, or agriculture which also restores important natural resources to benefit future farm families, their farms and communities.

Chapter 7: Barn raising covers appropriate methods for supporting the farm and community through initiatives that build assets – livestock pens, small-scale irrigation systems, greenhouses and grain silos, for example.

Chapter 8: Inspiring growth examines practical ways to support various farm-related business activities.

Chapter 9: Going to market describes the route that farm produce and products take on their way to the consumer. It highlights areas of particular importance in marketing, including pricing, competition and economic diversity.

Chapter 10: Banking on the family treats the subject of financial services for the farm family. It addresses savings and credit for crop and livestock production, asset creation and farm-related microenterprise activities.

Chapter 11: Speaking truth to power examines the importance of advocacy in rural development. It highlights a few critical issues and explains how organizations can best work together to advocate on behalf of marginalized and silent farm families.

Chapter 12: Breaking the rules is a very brief review of situations where advice prescribed in Chapters 5–10 is best ignored. Farms suffering from disease, drought, floods, earthquakes and war are in crisis. Assisting these farms may require interventions very different from those discussed in the rest of this book.

Each chapter follows a similar format, as follows:

- **Highlights:** Each chapter begins with a short list of the main points covered in the chapter.
- **Shaded boxes:** Each chapter contains short summaries of development successes and failures. The accounts in these boxes illustrate points made in the body of the text.
- **Take home messages:** Each chapter ends with a few key thoughts.

PART I

Understanding the resilient family farm

CHAPTER 1

Farm families and their social environment

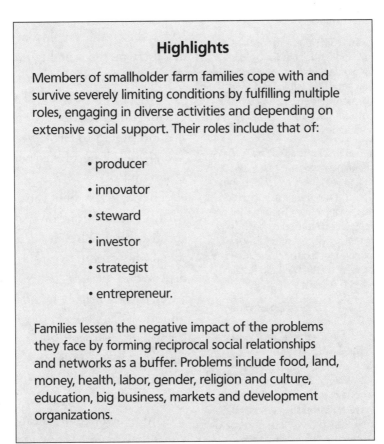

Highlights

Members of smallholder farm families cope with and survive severely limiting conditions by fulfilling multiple roles, engaging in diverse activities and depending on extensive social support. Their roles include that of:

- producer
- innovator
- steward
- investor
- strategist
- entrepreneur.

Families lessen the negative impact of the problems they face by forming reciprocal social relationships and networks as a buffer. Problems include food, land, money, health, labor, gender, religion and culture, education, big business, markets and development organizations.

Who are the smallholder farm families?

You have seen these families. They are the women who rise early and go to bed late so they have enough time to wash clothes in the stream, search for wild medicinal herbs, spend hours grinding millet into flour and care for young children and aging parents. They are the men who prepare small, disperse plots for planting – borrowing a water buffalo from one neighbor and a plow from another, digging ditches to keep rainwater away from chicken coops or traveling hundreds of kilometers to work as day laborers on pineapple plantations during the hunger season. You have seen these families tending fields on the farthest reaches of rural villages, removed from essential services of potable water, healthcare and schools. Often they reside on plots of land at desert margins or high along the slopes of steep mountains, littered with rocks, prone to wind erosion, difficult to level for planting and subject to harsh weather. We are speaking of the poorest farm families.

They cope as best they can, partly by building and diversifying social capital. They hold many social and productive roles and depend on a social safety net of relatives, friends, neighbors and communities. The Lopez family regularly shares fish from their pond with the Perez family, and when prolonged drought dries up the pond, the Perez family shares mangoes from their tree and meat from a goat they are forced to slaughter.

Their multiple roles

The small rural farming system is multi-faceted and dynamic, causing the farm family to balance many roles – producer, innovator, entrepreneur and steward – to name a few.

Farmer scientists

A clever NGO in the mountains of Kerala in southern India seeks out 'positive deviant' farmers who have innovated successfully and then helps the family to spread their innovation throughout local farm communities.

One family wanted to earn income by keeping bees that produced a rare and valuable medicinal honey. But each time the family tried to extract honey from the hive, the colony was disturbed or destroyed. The family noticed that in the wild, bees constructed their hives in three chambers, so the husband duplicated these divisions artificially.

Using three coconuts, he scraped out the white nutmeat, connected the shells in a verticle stack with small holes and string between each shell. He placed a queen inside. When it came time to collect the honey, the family simply removed the top shell where the honey collected without disturbing the colony in the other chambers.

This invention cost only coconuts and twine. Other families now hang ten or more hives under the eaves of their homes for dramatic increases in household income.

The NGO spreads news of advances like this one to local farm families by setting up demonstrations in strategic village locations.

Farm family as producer and scientist

To succeed as producers in limiting environments, where they are cultivating crops and raising livestock in spite of adversity and change, farm families respond by taking on the role of innovator. They use trial and error to test different ways of increasing the flow of water to crops, deterring insects and rodents from ripening grain plots or fattening goats more quickly. Out of necessity, many farmers experiment with traditional farming methods to improve on the past for today's challenges – to stem the impact of drought, take advantage of heavy rains, control persistent weeds, limit the damage of fire or preserve precious topsoil.[1]

Farm family as steward and investor

A variety of important resources lie in the custody of the farm family. They must protect their financial resources, often savings, in the form of cash, seeds and livestock. The farm family is also charged with protecting and restoring the farm's natural resources – water, soil and trees – for the benefit of the family and future families. Also under care of the farming family are the members of the family. Their health and education are essential to the work of the farm.

Protecting and allocating resources are activities that form the center of the small farm economy. Distributing expenses and investments comes with the farmer's role as steward. A family finds itself carefully balancing an investment in a long-term crop such as mahogany or teak with an investment in a small grain silo or payment of school fees.

Farm family as coping strategist and consumer

Farm families must manage a range of pressures arising from outside the farm, which continually influence the farm's success or threaten its survival. Neighbors, climate and counterproductive local

---

[1] Smallholder farming systems are based on a continual process of evaluating, experimenting and improving. Adapting to current challenges in a dynamic world is part of agriculture and farming. Given this cycle of innovation, traditional methods are not frozen in time, but change with each generation. It is important that development organizations not idealize traditional methods just because they are traditional. We may do farmers a disservice by failing to acknowledge and encourage farmers in their role as farmer scientists. Nor should we overlook our own role in linking farmers to appropriate innovations, information or technology that could resolve local problems.

customs can support or destroy the family farm. Unfavorable government policies or erratic markets can also weigh heavily on the farm family. Negative policies on competitive goods, taxation on land or income-generating activities and unfavorable pricing and subsidies can affect the survival of the small farm.

Farm families are often thought of only as producers who benefit from high prices. They are also consumers of agricultural inputs, tools, clothes and food. Unduly high prices may help the sellers, but hurt the many buyers who are often smallholder farm families themselves.

Not so sweet

When government pricing polices favored sugar imports, small farmers growing sugar cane in western Kenya faced a crisis. These policies depressed the market for local sugar products, leaving small farmers destitute. In order to survive, successful farmers quickly diversified into other high-value crops like cotton.

Farm family as opportunity seeker and entrepreneur

To prosper, the farm family must turn its attention to opportunities in the local community, as well as to the wider world of markets and trends. The family must understand the demand for its farm produce, the price each crop and animal might fetch and must balance these factors with the cost of production. It must understand the role of vegetable production in generating income and improving household nutrition. It must also understand effective crop management methods, new breeds of livestock, disease-resistant crops or low-cost water harvesting.

The farm family also seeks other services to increase or protect its own savings and investments. The entrepreneurial family wants credit to invest in a new opportunity or insurance to protect its crop.

Millet in Mali

In a village in Mali, men were migrating more and more, seeking work to supplement family income. The hunger season was lasting three months a year. Women farmers could not increase their production because the men were not available to help.

To cope, they built small metal silos to store millet, their primary crop. This effectively increased their yield by one third. Now their hunger season lasts only one month.

The social impact of the issues they face[1]

The problem of food

'We depend on the sky,' says a Cambodian farmer. 'If it rains, our rice fields are watered and we have a good harvest. If it does not, we go hungry for part of the year.'

Many of the world's rural farms and families depend on the sky. Their agriculture is rain-fed. No rain, no crop. No rain, no livestock.

Cambodia

The poorest families also face the added challenge of farming on the worst land – land to which they are relegated because large landowners already have the best land or because of expanding villages, new roads and larger rural communities. Food for these families is hard to come by. There is usually a hunger season, a period each year when food is so scarce that families reduce their food intake to one meal of rice or bananas a day.

To cope, they stretch their food supply by building silos, by drying or preserving food in jams, pickles and chutneys, by slaughtering livestock or by introducing income-generating activities during the off season. They depend on remittances from relatives who have migrated abroad or they buy food on credit from the local shopkeeper who trusts them because she knows them.

The problem of land

In some countries, the poorest families own no farmland and must sharecrop for wealthier landholders, offering a percentage of the harvest as payment for use of the land. Because the remainder is just enough food to meet the family's needs, they can sell no portion of

---

[1] The issues in this section are complex. Only a few key elements are highlighted for each problem. Although the list is not comprehensive, our intent is to introduce the idea that commonly faced problems have social impacts for farm families, impacts that may support, complicate or hinder a family's ability to cope.

the harvest. Without the possibility of converting the harvest into cash or cash into land, the farm family is tied perpetually to the landholder in a dependent, inequitable relationship.

In many countries, while farm families cultivate land that has belonged to them for generations, they do not hold formal title to the land, placing their shelter, assets and hard work at risk. In communities in Africa, ancestral land can be farmed, but is useless as collateral when the family needs a guarantee for credit. In other countries, there simply is not enough good land to go around, pushing the poorest farmers to the top of the watershed or the edge of the desert.

A resilient Central American farm: mixed maize–Mucuna–mahogany system

A mixed farming system that has had great success in Central America combines *Mucuna* species ('velvet bean') in no-till maize production. The velvet bean plants and residue cover the soil year-round (not shown in sketch), adding nitrogen and organic matter to the soil, outcompeting weeds and increasing maize yields. Pigs thrive on a 50:50 mix of maize and cooked *Mucuna*, reaching maturity and going to market more quickly than usual. Farmers plant high value hardwood trees every 7–8 meters among the maize plots, unconcerned that the trees will not mature for 20–25 years, because they receive a nice annual income from the sale of pigs. Trees are pruned of lower branches so shade does not interfere with maize growth. The resilient family farm in this figure also has a fish pond, vegetable garden, small fruit orchard, bananas and coconuts that provide food and cash.

A resilient Central American farm: mixed maize–Mucuna–mahogany system

The problem of money

The poorest farm families use many forms of money. In Indonesia some remove a handful of rice each day from the family stores, setting it aside, protected, for later sale or use. This is money. In Vietnam and Zimbabwe some fatten a pig or goat, and when cash is needed for school fees or funerals, they sell the animal. This is money. In El Salvador some gather bricks over many years in anticipation of upgrading their shelter, but at any time, they can exchange their bricks for cash. This is money. In Honduras or India, some grow cedar or mahogany trees so that they may sell the precious wood one day to pay for a daughter's dowry or wedding. This is money. In the Gambia some convert harvests into gold and wear the jewelry. This is money. In Bolivia some help a neighbor dig a pond or build a house. This is also money.

Theft, floods, pests, disease, community strife and irresponsible consumption threaten this money. Thieves steal it, floods drown it, pests eat it, disease destroys it, husbands drink it. The poorest farm families are under constant pressure to protect their money, whether in the form of cash, social capital, stored grains, livestock, trees, gold or bricks.[1]

This 'money' can also be viewed as family savings. Poor families struggle to raise lump sums of cash to meet timebound deadlines for school fees, agricultural inputs, healthcare, weddings or funerals. These 'savings' are converted to cash when needed.

The problem of health

Good nutrition contributes directly to the health and productivity of the farm family. Many of the poorest farm families produce a diet insufficient to nurture children, resist disease or provide the energy needed to perform multiple farming tasks. Adequate food with the right combination of nutrients may be unavailable because these families do not know efficient ways to grow a balanced diet, or because they must pay off high interest seed and fertilizer loans with

---

[1] Social capital is a complex mechanism that people use to cope with and adapt to change. It is defined by the World Bank as 'the norms and networks that enable collective action. …It is the glue that holds [a society] together.' Social cohesion is essential for economic growth and sustainable development. For more on social capital, see the World Bank website at www.worldbank.org/poverty/scapital. Also refer to World Bank Report 21936, Deepa Narayan et al., *Voices of the Poor: Crying out for Change*, 2000 and Report 20246, Deepa Narayan et al., *Voices of the Poor: Can Anyone Hear Us?* 2000.

Harvesting a balanced diet

In Cambodia, many families depend solely on food from harvesting rice and fish grown in the paddies. They lack year-round protein as the rains will produce only one harvest per year, leaving the paddies dry and without fish for many months. Although families store and use fermented fish paste during the dry season, it often runs out before the rainy season begins.

Thanks to a new project, families have introduced small livestock and vegetable gardens into their farms. They plant bamboo, fruit trees and *Acacia* for food, wood and as a natural fertilizer. They have year-round fish ponds, harvesting tilapia and two kinds of carp. Now they have protein and important vitamins and minerals year-round. They also receive cash from the sale of livestock and bamboo.

meager harvests, or because they lack sufficient land to grow the food they need. Important nutrients, particularly essential protein, vitamin A and iron, may be out of reach. Far from the advice of health workers and agricultural assistance, the poorest families have the least information and fewest resources needed to produce a balanced diet.

Clean, potable water is often far from easy reach. Village wells, if they exist, can be a long walk for those who live on the outskirts of communities. During a drought, people often have to drink from the same contaminated source as livestock. In India, members of one caste may restrict the use of wells by other castes.

The problem of labor

The farm family relies on its own labor force and that of neighbors to power its activities. Although some families own draft animals, the poorest do not. Family labor transforms scrubland into cropland, rain into small reservoirs and animals into assets. Family labor is connected to the number, age, health and availability of family members able to work.

The rhythm of family labor suffers when an adult leaves the farm to earn day wages elsewhere, while the spouse is left to manage the farm. The farm suffers when

Pitching in

Sisiket, Thailand. To make optimal use of labor, families carefully allocate each task to an appropriate family member. Adults prepare and harvest the fields. Children collect quail eggs and low-hanging fruit before school. Grandparents spin silk, weave mats and make incense.

firewood is scarce and a child must walk miles each day to gather fuel, or when water is scarce and the woman must walk miles for drinking water, or when good health is scarce and the family must use most of its energy to care for sick members.

Educated children are often a goal of the farm family. The family suffers when it must take its children out of school to work the farm. Worse still is when young boys remain in school, but young girls are taken out to carry water or mind younger children, widening the gender gap.

The problem of gender

Many rural societies have highly specialized roles for males and females. Custom may dictate which spouse tends small livestock (often women), which tends cattle and other grazing animals (often men), which cultivates the fields, which plants, weeds, harvests, threshes, grinds or sells.

While such division of labor can be a simple blueprint that helps family members allocate labor, often these specific roles rob women of important opportunities and decisions. For example, in rural Pakistan many women do not inherit the assets of the farm upon the death of the husband, as the plows, land and large animals are passed on to sons or other male next of kin. In southern Africa, key decisions are usually the province of the husband, including which crops to plant, what quantities to store and which investments to make.

Borrowing money and allocating household resources is often the

Cambodia

domain of men. Women may purchase food, pay school fees, buy medicine and clothes, yet the man may decide the amount to be spent for these purposes.

When a woman suddenly finds herself in the role of head of a household, through widowhood after war or seasonal migration by men for work, as an example, she faces a double crisis. She may find herself lacking the labor once provided by her husband, while facing decisions she has not had experience making. Her new demanding roles can place the small family farm in crisis, especially if she must focus on protecting and providing for her children.

On the other hand, once in a position to make decisions, women often seem to innovate and adapt more quickly than men, perhaps out of necessity to compensate for the lost labor or out of a stronger focus on the family and a greater desire to improve children's well-being.

The problem of education

Weighing the harvest, reading instructions on a half-kilo tin of seeds or counting cash to pay school fees are part of daily farm life. But what does the farm family do when no member can read the markings on a balance scale? Or when the planting instructions on a seed tin are critical to good results? Or when the family believes it has saved enough for school only to find it did not add the bills correctly? Literacy is not simply a route out of poverty, it is essential to basic survival.

Many countries have insufficient educational opportunities for both children and adults. Adding to the problem is the need

Where there's a will...

Andhra Pradesh, India. Tired of waiting for government services and oppressed by a caste system that did not allow their particular caste to attend the village school, women in a rural village pooled their savings for several years. They used the funds to build a schoolhouse and hire a teacher. The school is near the rice fields where these women spend most of their time, which makes minding their children before and after school possible.

of the farm family to direct part of its labor force to spend time away from the farm. Worse still, the poorest families are so far removed from educational facilities that children simply cannot make the journey to and from school within the existing daylight hours. In some areas, school fees are expensive, as are uniforms and books, limiting the number of children that farm parents can send to school, if any.

The problem of religion and culture

While religious and cultural customs are a great benefit to many villagers, some find themselves adversely affected by surrounding belief systems and cultural practices. The practice of one neighbor may affect the situation of another. For example, one religion may forbid handling pork, another killing cows, still another killing insects. In countries where neighbors represent a variety of religions, practices can differ widely, causing conflict. Compounding the problem are the issues of tribe, caste and ethnicity, where roles are clearly defined and may limit the variety of activities required to run a successfully resilient farm.

Good neighbors

Java, Indonesia. Christian farmers discovered that raising pigs was a profitable way to complement other farming activities. Whenever pigs escaped on the Christian Sabbath (a day of no work) into the yards of Muslims (who are not permitted to touch pigs), the Christian and Muslim farmers resolved their mutual problem by agreeing to pay Hindus to capture and return the lost pigs. The Hindus were pleased with the opportunity to earn extra income.

The problem of big business and big farms

Of increasing concern to farm families are large business operations that produce goods like soap, rope and candles to sell in villages. In the past, local farms made and sold these products to other villagers. Shifting the processing and post-harvest activities to big business removes scarce cash from the village economy, leaving fewer alternatives for generating income.

Farm families can lessen the impact of the loss of these economic activities by finding links to larger businesses and seeking their own market niches – supplying specialty raw materials or completing labor-intensive steps in the production process, for example. However, smallholder farmers may lack the information, confidence or negotiating skills to approach large businesses and farmers. This highlights a potential role for development organizations.

Large farms sharing land within the same watershed pose a threat as well. These operations often grow major commercial crops, using maximum amounts of water, chemical fertilizers, pesticides and herbicides. Runoff loaded with inorganic matter and toxic chemicals can contaminate surface and groundwater supplies, adversely affecting fish populations, water quality, crops and livestock of nearby family farms.

Increasing profits

The farm family can increase its profits in three ways, through:

1 **Increasing the price of goods sold** – through strategies like better packaging or storing grains until the market price increases.

2 **Increasing crop yield through improving the inputs** – increasing fertilizer applications, preparing or buying richer fertilizers or using improved seed varieties.

3 **Lowering the cost of production** – through strategies that increase efficiency and reduce risk. Using a cow to produce milk while also using its manure as fertilizer and cooking fuel is an example of efficiency. Building a simple water harvesting system on every rooftop to trap rainwater and offer the farm a second source of potable water is an example of risk reduction.

Most farm families believe they have more control over the third option and focus their efforts there. This opens the door for additional profits if families can begin to focus on the other options, as well.

The problem of markets

Smallholder farm families generally face unstable prices, prices over which they have little control and little information or warning. Of everything produced on a farm, the raw products are the least well paid. If farm families cannot market products they have processed themselves, they are unlikely to get decent returns.

Over the past several decades, the development community has been successful helping farm families increase production in environmentally sound ways, but they have been weak at supporting farmers in marketing, commercialization and value-added processing. With increasing globalization of markets, small farmers are likely to become increasingly marginalized without support in this arena.

The problem of development organizations

Thousands of local and international organizations dedicate their services to assisting the poorest farm families. Advisers sometimes devise interventions that prove risky and can be devastating to small farm livelihoods. When these schemes require the family to move away from the best elements of the traditional practices that sustained the farm in the past into new, unproven technologies, they create new pressures on the farming system. Neither traditional nor modern methods alone are apt to resolve all the challenges of smallholder farming systems. Some combination, locally tested and adapted, often works best.

Untested interventions promoted and implemented with great enthusiasm ignore the reality of the smallest family farms. While they give the organization or adviser a chance to see his or her schemes put into action and bestow a feeling of usefulness on the organization or adviser, seemingly benign projects can have destructive consequences and place the family farm at risk. They can also set a community against accepting development assistance ever again.

One of the greatest weaknesses of the support given to small farmers by development organizations has been the lack of systematic, but

Bees without blossoms

Darkabir, Turkey. In southern Turkey, a local organization decided that honey production was a good activity for poor farmers in villages situated on rocky plains near the Tigris. The organization set families up with beehives, the cost of which was to be repaid in jars of honey that the organization would sell. Farmers discovered there were not enough flowers with the pollen that attracted the bees near the village, so they piled the hives on horse-drawn carts and hauled the bees many kilometers to a site with more of the favored flowers. Even these efforts proved fruitless.

The farmers, enraged that they had altered their farming patterns to accommodate the meddling organization, refused to pay for the hives with honey that the bees could not produce. The farmers destroyed the hives.

reasonable evaluation and assessment that can provide feedback during implementation, identify successes and failures and provide information about the reasons for each. Our failure to collect the necessary data, engage in critical self-analysis and share evaluation results means wasted resources as we reinvent the wheel and continue making similar mistakes. We often have very little proof, one way or the other, of the impact of our work.

Take home message

Smallholder farm families cope with and compensate for the challenges of multi-faceted, limiting environments by filling multiple social roles, by depending on complex social networks and by engaging in reciprocal social relationships.

Ecuador

CHAPTER 2

Farm families and their natural environment

Highlights

Farmers find many ways to minimize constraints and maximize the benefits of natural resources for agriculture, while protecting them for future use. This chapter covers water, soil, wind, sun, fire, weeds and pests.

The importance of farm resources

Out of necessity, the poorest farm families must make every available resource work to its fullest measure. Natural resources on or near the family farm are the least costly resources for the farmer to deploy for farm use. They are close at hand and offered by nature at no cost except labor, which can be the most abundant resource on family farms. Moreover, these natural resources can often generate better results than their synthetic substitutes.

The challenge for the farm family is to wring from every drop of water and every inch of soil its full productive potential, while ensuring that the same supply of water and same quality of soil are available for coming harvests.

This double task requires that the family farm the land with an eye to the preservation and replenishment of naturally available resources. Poor water management may lead to a contaminated or inadequate water supply and can worsen the impact of drought. Poor soil fertility management can lead to harvests with successively lower yields. Both have the effect of robbing the family of its chances for survival and prosperity.

Environmental problems

The problem of water

Water, sun, air and soil are the lifeblood of the family farm. Water, in particular, affects all aspects of farm life, from the health of the family to cultivation of crops and raising of animals. In order to mature, plants and animals need clean, plentiful water devoid of contaminants and salts.

Water is also a people issue. People use it, dam it, channel it, pollute it, waste it, deplete it and fight over it. When water is scarce, people's activities can heighten the impact of scarcity. Farm families can lower water tables through improper cultivation, wasteful use or poor irrigation techniques. Droughts magnify the problem. Lowered water tables may have a serious effect on farming activities. Crop root systems struggle to reach the water table, plants wither, land sinks, rivers and springs dry up. As streams and irrigation channels shrink into puddles, standing water accumulates, multiplying disease and pest problems.

Ecuador

In many countries, the poorest farm families, dependent on rainfed agriculture, are driven to the upper reaches of watersheds at and beyond the extreme margins of land that is suitable for agriculture. These farmers inhabit those areas of slopes and depressions down which rain and spring-fed rivers and streams travel. Diverting water to irrigate upland farms may deprive larger farms and wealthier landowners below of their expected supply. Farmers in the valleys often expect the poorest farmers on steep slopes and ridges to protect the supply of water that originates at the top of the watershed by careful use and by maintaining protective vegetative cover. However, they

Aerial view of a micro-watershed

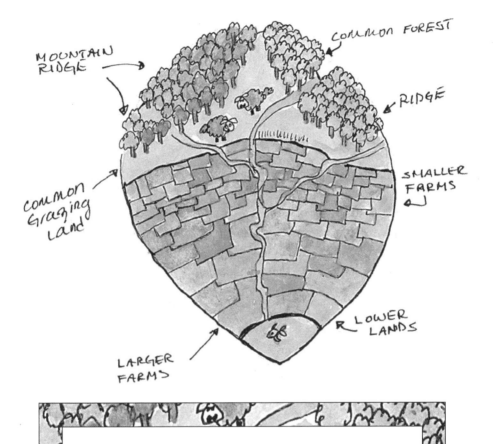

MOUNTAIN RIDGE

COMMON FOREST

RIDGE

SMALLER FARMS

common Grazing Land

LARGER FARMS

R LOWER LANDS

Aerial view of a micro-watershed

This figure shows an aerial view of a micro-watershed. While a watershed is the entire catchment area of a river system, a micro-watershed is one of many smaller sub-catchment areas that drain into feeder streams for the main waterway. Watershed or micro-watershed borders form an invisible line linking the highest elevation points that ring the watershed. These high points cause all water to flow towards the stream or river. The figure shows that land use at the top of the watershed is primary forest and pastureland, with farm plots located at middle and lower elevations.

A micro-watershed

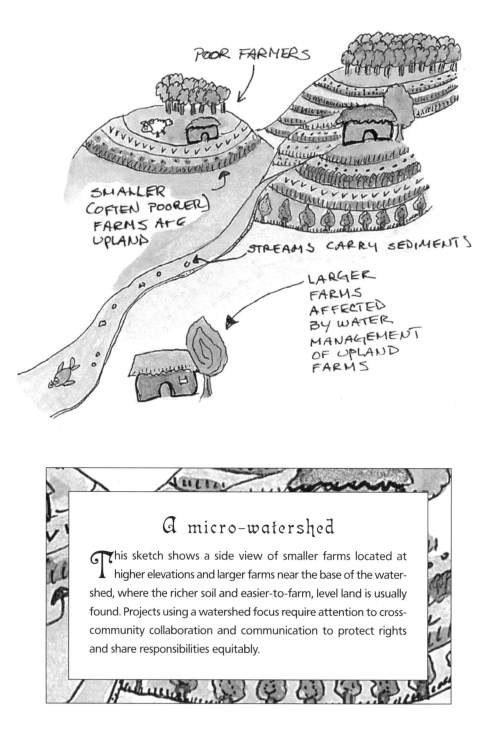

POOR FARMERS

SMALLER (OFTEN POORER) FARMS ATE UPLAND

STREAMS CARRY SEDIMENTS

LARGER FARMS AFFECTED BY WATER MANAGEMENT OF UPLAND FARMS

A micro-watershed

This sketch shows a side view of smaller farms located at higher elevations and larger farms near the base of the watershed, where the richer soil and easier-to-farm, level land is usually found. Projects using a watershed focus require attention to cross-community collaboration and communication to protect rights and share responsibilities equitably.

rarely think of sharing the cost of planting trees. Social conflict may arise when the poorest are unable or unwilling to protect the water supply for the richest.

Farm families, including the very poorest families, manage the quality and quantity of water through various means. Their primary goal is to remove variability from their water supply, which is subject to the vagaries of climate and weather, while still maintaining good relations with neighbors.

To maintain a more consistent supply of water, farm families work hard to capture and store water during the rainy season for use during the dry season. Vessels near gutters catch rainwater close to the home, as do roofs that are shaped like a basin. Ponds and small dams along streams hold and store water. Good soil management and cropping patterns help ensure that water is continuously available to different plants throughout the growing season. Simple irrigation systems help the farm family weather the dry season.

The problem of soil

Soil is alive. It is a complex, virtually invisible system of inorganic sand, silt, and clay; the organic remains of plants and animals; and millions of tiny, living organisms. With the help of larger creatures like earthworms and beetles, these micro-organisms break down dead plant and animal matter, mixing it with particles of soil so that important nutrients are stored where they are available to plants as roots need them.

The kitchen sink

In Guatemala, farm families build their compost heaps with eggshells that provide calcium, kitchen scraps and maize leaves that provide essential carbon and trace elements, chicken manure that is high in nitrogen and ash from cooking fires that provides potassium and phosphorous. When decomposed, this compost provides a natural time-release fertilizer that is richer and more complete than purchased, inorganic fertilizer.

Soil scientists say that one inch (2.54 centimeters) of topsoil, the fertile, loamy soil on which crops thrive, takes about one hundred years to develop through natural processes. By its very nature, the work of cultivating land for agriculture exposes and degrades precious topsoil. Many cultivation practices leave land bare until

35

plants grow and develop a canopy, exposing the soil to the effects of wind, rain and too much sun. In addition, crops require large quantities of nutrients. These nutrients, pulled up through the roots during the growing season, leave the field with the harvest, permanently spent, unless somehow replaced.

The poorest families, whether farming the top of a steep watershed, or working the fringes of a relatively flat farming community, usually farm the most degraded soils – rocky soils, clay soils, salty, sandy or infertile soils. Excessive clay means plant roots will be trapped or suffocate. Soils with lots of clay become waterlogged when it rains, and the heavy clay blocks roots from growing easily, from reaching nutrients and finding essential oxygen. On the other hand, in excessive sand, plants will either starve or die of thirst. Sandy soils are generally infertile, and they drain water so quickly and easily that it's gone before plants can use it. When a soil has too many rocks or gravel, seeds have trouble germinating and roots have trouble growing. When farmers irrigate a lot, but do not flush and drain the soil from time to time, fertilizer salts collect at the surface and soil can become too saline for plant growth.

Can of worms

In Cuba, farm families cultivate containers of soil, kitchen garbage and earthworms, which they spread in fields to break down organic matter and improve soil structure. As worms digest leaves, and other organic matter, they accelerate the process of creating nutrient-rich soil and humus.

Farmers improve soil by increasing its fertility (amount of plant available nutrients), by providing a healthy environment for biological activity (microflora and microfauna), by improving its physical properties for root growth and by helping the soil to maintain a good balance between water retention and drainage. Farmers improve soil fertility by replacing

Green manure

In Peru, farm families cultivate 'leguminous' plants that are able to take nitrogen from the air and convert it into a form in the soil that other crops can use. Families turn young crops of tropical kudzu into the soil to increase its nitrogen content and improve its capacity to hold and drain water and even control weeds when cut and left to die on the surface. These nitrogen-fixing plants are called 'green manure'.

lost, harvested organic matter through composting, vermiculture (producing worms in a bed of manure) and by incorporating animal manure or green manure from high-nitrogen plants. Farm families create compost heaps made of organic matter readily available on the farm – ash, eggshells, leaves and straw, kitchen scraps and manure. Carefully constructed and maintained over several months, these compost heaps yield dark, crumbly, fresh-smelling matter that is called humus – the farmer's gold.

Humus is rich in nitrogen, phosphorous and potassium, the main nutrients needed for good plant growth, as well as many other important nutrients and trace elements. Humus adds fertility to sandy soils and helps retain water, it helps aerate and loosen clay soils and it provides habitat for the flora and fauna that keep the soil healthy and functioning. Humus is not simply farmer's gold, but soil's lifeblood.

The problem of wind, sun and fire

Wind racing unchecked across a freshly planted field can destroy young seedlings. It blows sand that destroys young leaves, it dries and withers them and removes topsoil. Wind can also harm crops in the middle of the growing season, making it difficult for plants to retain water, flattening and bending taller plants like maize or millet and exposing shorter crops like beans and sweet potatoes to the hot sun.

When wind removes rich topsoil, it can leave the land unproductive for future crops. It also increases the amount of labor the farm family must exert to remove dead plants and clean out low lying areas covered by soil. When livestock are allowed to overgraze pastureland or when forests are cut

Fire escape

Cashews produce tasty nuts to sell, but trees also serve as a natural firebreak. The tree's roots produce a mild herbicide that prevents grasses from growing beneath. If a fire approaches several rows of cashew trees, a stretch of bare ground breaks its spread.

back excessively, the land is deprived of a proper defense against the wind. With time, severe wind erosion, combined with overgrazing, overcultivation and deforestation, can and does lead to the formation of deserts.

Sunlight gives crops the energy they need to convert carbon dioxide and water into plant material. But too much sun, wind and heat

Gambia

can dry the soil and burn crops. Tropical farmers use a variety of tricks to cope with the harmful impact of sun and wind. Their goal is to create a favorable micro-climate, one that lowers or mod-ulates the temperature of the air and soil while preventing loss of precious water. Families can limit the power of wind by building windbreaks of trees planted in a row perpendicular to the wind's prevailing direction. Trees like *Acacia* and *Calliandra* serve well as this kind of protection. Families can also plant vegetative covers of bushy legumes and thick grasses in open fields to deal with the effects of both wind and sun. These canopies of growing plants hold the soil in place, protecting it from removal by wind and rain.

As with wind, farm families can protect crops in arid zones from too much sun. Farmers shade young plants by planting them between rows of trees in an alley cropping system, or they cover the surrounding soil with dead leaves, straw or cut grass as mulch to hold water in the soil and suppress weeds. Millet, maize and sorghum provide excellent canopies to shade low-growing crops such as sweet potatoes, cassava and beans. Farm families also plant trees that form living fences on plot borders like *Leucaena* for rich animal fodder prunings, trees for lumber and fruit or nut trees. Living fences also resist damage caused by termites and shade crops for part of the day.

Lightning, sun and people start fires. Fire, quite obviously, will destroy crops, animals and shelter. Fire is often used to clear land for farm-ing, as it is an easy way to rid an area of weeds and unwanted shrubs or trees. While kitchen ashes can nourish the soil when mixed with dead plant matter, so that nutrients are trapped in the rich, dark humus produced in compost piles, ashes that remain on the surface of the soil after a fire have short-lived benefits. They provide an imme-diate flush of nutrients to the soil, but they are easily washed or blown away, usually before new seedlings are large enough to make use of them.

The practice of clearing land through fire can do much harm. Fire burns the millions of micro-organisms that live near the soil surface. Their job is to break down undecomposed organic matter, so that important nutrients become available to crops. Fire also kills wildlife, birds, bees and beneficial soil creatures. It clouds the atmosphere with harmful smoke, and acrid air pollution can blanket entire regions for weeks as smoke particles block sunlight. Yet for many farm families, fire is the most effective tool they have to control weeds and pests. The trick is to burn judiciously and properly.

The farm family copes with fire through natural or manmade firebreaks or by keeping soil as moist as possible. Some trees resistant to fire can block its spread, others retard it by limiting the growth of grasses underneath.

The problem of the unwanted

Weeds compete with crops for soil, sun, water and nutrients. Rodents and birds seek the same yield from crops, growing or stored, as the farm family. Cutworms, locusts, beetles and weevils feed off the leaves, fruit and roots of crops, raid grain bins and food stores. Free-roaming goats trample vegetables in the gardens of neighbors, chew the crops of the farm family and destroy soil dikes and wood fences.

Diseases kill livestock, ruin crops and weaken members of the farm family.

Weeds, snakes, rats and insect pests are unwanted on the family farm. But as much as farmers might like, they will never disappear completely. Each has important functions in natural ecosystems. Botanists like to say that a weed is a plant whose purpose has not yet been discovered. Good

Small is beautiful

The humble radish is more than a food; the lowly garlic is more than a flavor enhancer. In Thailand, families intercrop radishes with cucumbers. The radishes repel cucumber beetles, protecting both crops. In many countries farmers use a spray of diluted garlic juice to kill bacteria that damage fruits, nuts and vegetables.

farming system management can prevent the unwanted from taking more than their fair share of the family farm.

What to do about the unwanted? Prevention is the chief strategy. To prevent weed growth, farmers will mulch between crop rows. Deprived of needed sunlight, many weed seeds never get the chance to sprout. Farmers also plant companion crops near primary ones. The roots, color or smell of the companion plants may deter weed growth or control disease or insect problems for the primary crop. Farmers also use commonly available items like vinegar or neem tree byproducts to kill weeds.

Dealing with harmful insects is another ceaseless task. Resourceful families often use cheaper natural methods to keep insect levels under control. They cultivate companion crops that attract predators to consume unwanted insects in the main crop. They mix a variety of organic pesticides to ward off persistent predators. Garlic and chili mixed with water deter insects from their rice feasts. Water from seeds of the neem tree is diluted into a spray that prevents pests from damaging the roots and stems of maize, tobacco and coffee.

Bug stew

In Liberia farmers fill a barrel with water and the remains of grasshoppers and crickets. After barrels sit for several days in the hot sun, farmers spray the bug stew on their cabbage fields. Crickets and grasshoppers, repelled by the scent of their ancestors, flee.

Farmers handpick large caterpillar pests and larvae from stems and leaves and use barriers to protect plants from pests. They string up nets to keep out birds and insects. To bar goats, they plant thorny shrubs. To keep snails and slugs at bay, women spread cooking fire ash on the soil in a ring around their vegetables, its grit preventing slugs from slithering toward plump tomatoes.

Disease can also damage crops. One strategy farmers use is to plant improved disease-resistant varieties, if they have the money. But often farm families do their own plant breeding by annual selection. They plant a field and choose the most resistant plants from each year's crop to provide seeds for the next crop. After repeatedly choosing the strongest plants, farmers are able to select resistant strains in sufficient quantities for entire fields of future crops.

Slug tavern

Farm families in Mexico were annoyed at the damage caused by slugs, who were fond of feasting in local vegetable gardens. Several families decided to test different deterrents. On Saturday mornings after a fiesta, people discovered how much slugs loved the leftover beer. Now they place beer in shallow bowls sunk to ground level near the crops. Slugs happily get drunk on the beer and drown.

Families also diversify the crops they plant near each other to stop the spread of disease. For example, they will plant two rows of maize interspersed with several rows of beans, or they will plant climbing beans or climbing squash in the same mounds with maize seed.

Diseases preferring one kind of host can have difficulty spreading past rows planted to other crops. Farmers also rotate crops to stave off diseases that lie dormant in the soil between growing seasons. If families plant onions in one plot this year and peas in the same plot next year, onion pathogens will die off for lack of a meal.

Take home message

The most resilient farm families combine short-term and long-term objectives, seeking a balance between production for today and conservation for tomorrow.

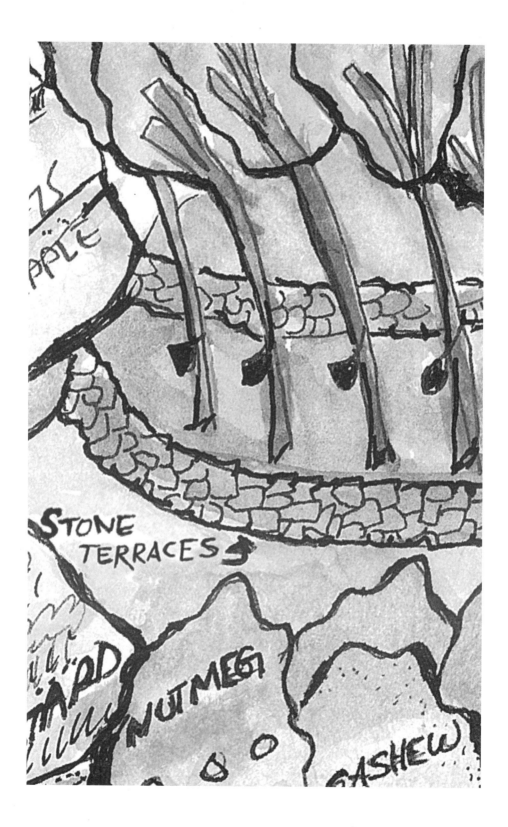

CHAPTER 3

The family farm as an agricultural system

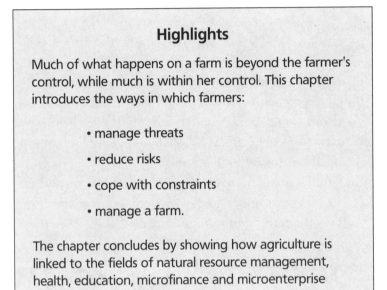

Highlights

Much of what happens on a farm is beyond the farmer's control, while much is within her control. This chapter introduces the ways in which farmers:

- manage threats
- reduce risks
- cope with constraints
- manage a farm.

The chapter concludes by showing how agriculture is linked to the fields of natural resource management, health, education, microfinance and microenterprise development.

The agricultural system

Small farm agricultural systems are production systems that are generally thought of as no more than 5 hectares (12 acres) in size, yet the poorest farm families have significantly less land, often only half a hectare (about one acre) located in highly disperse, separate parcels. Families manage these small farms to earn part or all of their livelihoods. They raise livestock and fish; grow crops, vegetables and trees; produce farm inputs like seeds, fish fingerlings and fodder; manage farm assets and natural resources; add value to farm products through post-harvest processing and sell surplus goods at Saturday market. In higher, cooler plots, families grow potatoes and coffee; in lower, dryer

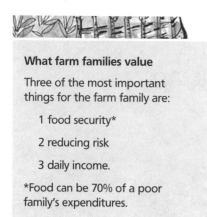

plots they grow millet and melons.

Families manage and coordinate activities and resources, flora and fauna, biochemical and physical processes. They manage soil processes, water and nutrient flows, solar and heat energy and modify micro-climates to the benefit of crops. They coordinate family labor, adjusting activities to seasonal weather cycles; participate in irrigation water user associations to manage benefits and responsibilities; they contribute to community work crews to level and bund moderate slopes so they can farm the land. They belong to community marketing cooperatives, village banks and PTAs (community support organizations for local schools).

Farm families maintain roads to get tools from town and crops to market, they borrow money to pay for seeds, they practice soil and water conservation, they innovate and test new ideas. They work hard

Resilient south India farm

This family's farming system includes diverse perennials (a few of each type of tree – coffee, cacao, banana, coconut palms, rubber, nuts, spice trees), annuals (rice, mustard, spices), tubers (yams, ginger) and livestock (dairy cow, pigs, poultry, fish). They produce biogas for cooking and heating, collect rainwater for cooking and drinking and produce medicinal honey in coconut hives for cash. By doing post-harvest processing of the raw materials they produce, they are able to fetch a higher price at the market. By producing many different things, they can be certain that if the price of one product is low, another will be high.

Resilient south India farm

COFFEE & CACAO
RUBBER
BANANA SAPLINGS
PINEAPPLE
STONE TERRACES
RICE
MUSTARD
NUTMEG
CASHEW
COW SHED
BIO-GAS
SLURRY
CHICKEN COOP
AFRICAN CATFISH
COMPOST
TAPIOCA
PEPPER
NATURAL FENCE
BEE HIVE
CARDAMOM
RUBBER
COCONUT SHELL
TURMERIC
YAMS
GINGER
RAIN WATER HARVESTING
SHALLOW WELL
COFFEE

at getting access to suitable land. They seek information and moral support from neighbors and agricultural extensionists.

Farm families are multi-taskers and innovative entrepreneurs. They are also laborers, tillers, herders, researchers, ecologists, foresters, meteorologists, machinists, entomologists, nutritionists, veterinarians, construction engineers, carpenters, botanists and soil scientists.

Threats and risks

What happens on the farm is often out of the control of the farm family. For example, when a politically unstable government floods the market with cheap imported rice just before harvest, the farm family feels betrayed by its own government and cannot sell its surplus rice at a profit. However, the politicians and national government remain in power, because the masses of urban poor are fed.

In this example, if the farm family has been fortunate and wise, they or their community will have a grain silo to store surplus rice until prices rise. Or they may have mature fuelwood trees to harvest and sell or plump broilers ready for local markets. Or they will borrow money from the cousin who was given a gift of the goat's kid last year. If they are unwise or unlucky, they will borrow money from a loan shark at terms they cannot afford to pay back, sell the family goat or send the man of the house to a coastal sugar plantation to sell his labor cutting cane. If they are really desperate and have no other reserves, the family will begin to sell assets that compromise future earnings – a piece of land, the family plow or a small fruit orchard.

Achieving farming systems' goals is more than a finely tuned juggling act by experienced farm families. It involves multiple strategies to cope with multiple risks, and it is extremely difficult

One step at a time

In Orissa, India, farmers eager to increase their income are reluctant to invest in a standard-size chicken coop that houses many chickens. New chicken breeds allow farmers to get into the chicken business gradually.

Specially-bred free range chickens are able to forage for food unprotected in the farm yard and still fatten well. While their maturity takes a few months longer than caged chickens, cost of food and care is low. Plus their tasty meat brings a good price. Farm families can invest in 10–20 chickens at a time without too much risk.

without supportive or at least benign national policy and weather. It is impossible or nearly impossible during wars, natural disasters, economic crashes, locust plagues or in areas where there are high rates of HIV/AIDS.

Reducing risk

Although farm families cannot control off-farm factors, there is much that they can control. By maintaining diverse farming systems, they can secure their well-being and maintain survival even in moderately unstable environments. They can minimize risk with different productive activities, spread multiple, heavy labor requirements throughout the year and diversify and improve the family diet and family income. If the family has the labor, resources and knowledge to manage the farm properly, they can protect, recycle and make efficient use of the natural resource base.

Improving productivity (increasing the production per unit area of land) is increasingly important for today's rural poor, as family plot size shrinks from generation to generation. Generally, on a worldwide scale, production can no longer be increased through felling forest margins to create new pastures and cropland or through breeding higher-yielding varieties. There are no new lands available for agriculture, and breeders have reached plant physiological limits for yield increases of key grains.

What goes around comes around

In South-east Asia farmers have perfected an intensive pig–fish production system. A pigpen with a cement floor drains directly into an adjacent fish pond, providing natural pig fertilizer to the pond. This fertilizer feeds the plankton that feeds the fish. It fertilizes the miracle duckweed that feeds the pig and keeps the pond clean for the fish.

Vegetables and ipil ipil (*Leucaena* spp.) trees thrive on the pond banks in the moist, rich soil. Ipil ipil leaves fall into the pond, feed the fish, fertilize the pond and provide cut-and-carry fodder for the pig.

On their royal diets of rice bran, vegetables, beans, ipil ipil and duckweed, pigs become bacon very quickly, feeding the farmer who feeds the pig who feeds the fish.

Food security solutions for the future tend to lie not with increasing food production through allocating increased land to agriculture (extensification), but through higher productivity (intensification) on each plot of agricultural land, using higher levels of inputs or seeking greater efficiencies in the use of resources and inputs. This includes recycling and rehabilitating resources, curbing resource use, reducing resource waste or increasing the use of inputs like fertilizer and high-yielding varieties.

Taking water as an example, farmers in semi-arid regions can make the most of scarce water by planting fast-maturing crops or varieties that use less water. They can replace cash crops that are heavy water users like sugar cane with low water users like cotton. They can plant drought-tolerant trees that yield fruit or nuts with little water. They can manage the soil so it holds water longer, using mulches and tilling the soil in ways that seal the surface and prevent evaporation. They can copy or develop clever ways of collecting and storing rooftop water or rain that falls on sloped land.

Coping with constraints – the big three

Constraint 1 – water

In many areas of the world, the major constraint for the poorest farm families is water. Far too often, farmers in Africa, Asia and Latin America now say that rainfall amounts are significantly less than they were 20 years ago, when their land supported upland rice or bananas. Now they must plant cassava, cotton, sorghum and millet, because these crops require less rain. Too often, farmers also say rainfall is much less dependable. The rainy season begins in fits and starts, onset can be delayed a month or more and the initial soaking rains that signal planting time are followed by three weeks of sun, withering and killing seedlings.

Farmers cope with variable weather patterns in ingenious ways. Honduran farm families use microfinance loans to buy cement for one cubic meter micro-reservoirs buried to ground level and spaced along the contour. Once filled, these small 'tanks' supply enough liquid to hand-water seedlings, taking the guesswork out of early planting. Families not only plant, but harvest, a month earlier than their neighbors, getting better market prices and planting their second crop sooner.

Constraint 2 – land

Often, the critical constraint facing small farm families is land. Families can be very creative in maximizing land use, availing themselves of all three dimensions, not just the top layer of soil that forms the surface area of their plots.

Vertical space becomes important. In Cambodia, tall, narrow palms that produce useful sap are staggered on paddy bunds without reducing needed light for rice. Vietnamese families develop multi-story systems where tall and medium-height trees are spread among crop fields of tall grain crops interplanted with bushy tomatoes or climbing beans.

Farmers and agronomists test and refine these multi-story systems to find plant combinations and spacings that work well. Otherwise, competition for water, light and nutrients can easily reduce productivity or increase disease.

Depth also becomes important. In Pakistan, farmers bury mushroom sheds in the ground of soils that are not suitable for planting. Storage structures are placed on top of mushroom sheds for greater land-use efficiency.

Constraint 3 – labor

In other areas, labor is the major constraint for small farms. An area may be less densely populated because it is remote or has a harsh climate, because of high emigration rates or because of decimation from war or disease. In Zimbabwe, where many adults have died of HIV/AIDS, farm families plant community gardens, sharing labor, using increased fossil fuel inputs like bagged fertilizer when possible, supplementing their labor and increasing productivity under difficult circumstances. While still active, HIV-positive adults are building fish ponds, planting fruit orchards and constructing beehives to ensure their young children have low-labor ways to survive once orphaned.

Elements of agricultural systems

While there is much that farm families cannot control, they do have control over how they manage their farming systems. By keeping their systems diverse, the farm family decreases risk. If a vegetable crop fails, chances are the fruit trees will bear fruit, the fish pond will yield fish or the bee hives honey. Diverse systems also allow the family to share or spread labor. Different farm activities require different amounts of effort over the year or season. During harvest, the family may have little time for collecting and selling honey. But in the off season, honey can become a significant time investment and income-producing activity for the family.

Families can decide how to use the land; which crop, tree and livestock combinations to plant in which cropping patterns; whether to use mechanical, botanical or chemical methods of pest control; whether to stagger plantings for ongoing harvests and market sales; whether to focus on high-value, perishable vegetable crops because the farm is close to markets; or whether to plant non-perishable 'dry beans', because the farm is remote and products must be transported long distances.

They manage elements and processes, contribute labor, adjust to change and innovate. They manage seasons, time and micro-climates to their benefit, modifying soil surfaces to deal with too much or too little water, too high or too low temperatures. They reshape landscapes to make agriculture easier or more productive. But above all, they make trade-offs and seek alternatives.

The old boy network

In the 1970s in the Gambia, Green Revolution extension workers wanted to increase rice yields in the lowlands. Traditionally, lowlands were the only farmland women owned. The rice the women produced from these paddies was the sole source of income they could offer their families.

The agronomists and extension workers, all male, trained the husbands on new Green Revolution techniques, ignoring traditional divisions of labor that complemented traditional farming systems. They also provided the men with tools and fertilizer.

The men took over the lowland rice paddies, leaving women with no income to offer the family and no assets over which they had control. To this day, women must seek permission to farm the remaining land with other crops.

Obvious elements in a farming system are the farm family, their pastures, fishponds, irrigation systems, sorghum and cassava plots, eucalyptus and banana trees, manure heaps, ducks and rabbits. Other farming system elements are not as obvious – the manual oilseed press, the wooden threshing tools, the dimestore calculator. Some elements are even less noticeable – processes that take place in the soil and in plants to support or inhibit plant growth, loss of precious nitrogen to the air when plants are burned or when manure is left on the soil surface. Whether obvious or not, they all must be used and managed wisely and productively in the successful resilient family farm.

Synergy between agriculture and natural resources

Stewardship of resources, the farm's natural capital, ensures a base for future productivity. It also creates natural synergies that foster efficiencies in the farming system. Although many families are in a desperate fight to provide one or two meals a day, blocking attention to anything else, there are others who are not as desperate and who see themselves as conservers and protectors of the natural resources on which their livelihoods depend.

For example, families who plant live barriers of trees along the contour lines of sloped plots prevent losses of topsoil gold. Live barriers increase the amount of water that infiltrates the soil in dry regions or sloped plots, increasing crop yield and recharging underground sources. With more water, plants grow faster, becoming stronger and more

Guatemala

resistant to stress earlier in the growing season, reducing crop loss due to harsh weather, pests or disease.

Tree branches in live barriers can be pruned, decreasing pressure  on local forests for fuelwood. Leaves can be used for green manure, mulch and fodder, enriching nearby soils, conserving soil moisture and providing high-protein animal fodder. Improving the quality and quantity of livestock feed allows the farm to raise more and healthier livestock. It creates additional manure for composting and provides animal power to cultivate more deeply and increase yields through intensification, or till more land and increase yields through extensification. In addition, mixed crop systems use water, sun and nutrients more efficiently. All these practices increase crop production, yield surpluses, strengthen farm resilience, and improve food security and family income.

Though not the topic of this book, healthy, robust natural resource systems are essential to mitigating the negative impact of natural disasters and reducing emergency recovery costs. Hurricane Mitch in Central America was only average in rainfall intensity, quantity and duration. Yet damage in Honduras was severe, in large part because of widespread deforestation and already saturated soils throughout this mountainous country of 85% sloped lands.

Agricultural synergy with education, health and microfinance

Other sectors, such as health, education and financial services, complement agriculture to help farm families achieve their goals. While the goal of the resilient farm family is to achieve an optimum balance between productive outputs, profits, resource protection and food security, the family cannot achieve its goals without information or the skills associated with good health, proper education or reliable financial resources.

Agriculture and education

In order to weigh alternatives and make good management decisions, farmers need some of the skills that scientists use in order to innovate and test alternatives. Simple methods and tools are available to help farmers experiment and evaluate results. But these methods require basic reading and math skills, and adults in poor farm families are often illiterate.

Although adult literacy is essential to resilient farms, general adult literacy programs have not attained widespread success. However, when lessons are targeted to specific, immediate goals like recognizing, recording and adding numbers on a tin-can rain gauge or totaling harvest weights from a balance scale and calculating market prices, literacy training can be highly effective. Once learned, these skills have a domino effect in self-esteem and pride, strengthening the community's water user associations and village banks, for example.

Agriculture health and nutrition

Training for farm family members in health and nutrition helps them grow a balanced diet, making wise decisions about the most nutritious crops to plant, the importance of variety in diet and the right combinations of foods to reduce child malnutrition and lengthen the productive life of adults with HIV/AIDS. Health/nutrition training strengthens the farm family for productive work and increases farming system diversity for greater food security.

Agriculture, microfinance and microenterprise

Access to flexible savings and credit services (microfinance) allows farm families to increase productive assets and respond to market opportunities (microenterprise and business development). Training in simple market analysis and access to marketing information can mean increased income, especially when these microenterprise activities complement microfinance services. When further complemented by adult literacy and health activities, microfinance and microenterprise activities strengthen all aspects of the family farm, securing well-being even in unfavorable environments.

Meat on their bones

In a mountain village in the Philippines, nutritionists and agronomists teamed up to eradicate severe malnutrition forever.

The agronomists helped families double their rice yields and plant fast-growing fuelwood trees. Nutritionists taught villagers not to polish the rice, which gets rid of the outer bran layer, where the protein and nutrition are located. Polishing turns 'brown' rice, or whole grain rice, into white rice, but white rice has only carbohydrates. When combined with beans, nuts, seeds or green leafy vegetables, whole grain rice provides complete protein in the diet, regardless of whether meat is available.

After the project, villagers watched children's bellies shrink and body weights soar, while children in surrounding villages who were still eating white rice struggled with high rates of malnutrition.

A word of caution – microfinance institutions have not had great success adding microenterprise services to their savings and credit services. It may be wiser to let separate institutions support the same communities, providing different, but complementary, services.

Take home message

Family farms are beset by complex challenges and constraints. Resilient farms resist threats and stress through diverse solutions, skilled management and clever stewardship of scarce resources.

AIDS farmer near orphans' fish pond, Zimbabwe

CHAPTER 4

The family farm as an economic system

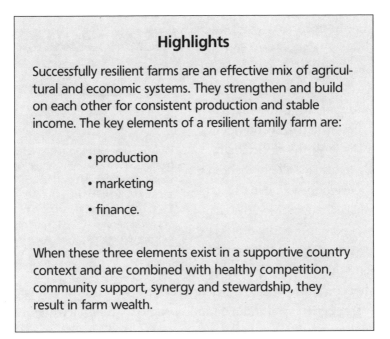

Highlights

Successfully resilient farms are an effective mix of agricultural and economic systems. They strengthen and build on each other for consistent production and stable income. The key elements of a resilient family farm are:

- production

- marketing

- finance.

When these three elements exist in a supportive country context and are combined with healthy competition, community support, synergy and stewardship, they result in farm wealth.

The economic system

Women sell cassava flatbread carefully processed and slow-baked to get rid of naturally occurring cyanide, they sell candles made of beeswax from family hives located near the village eucalyptus grove or they sell tea from hibiscus bushes that border their homes. Men sell lumber made from the fast-growing trees lining their sorghum and maize plots or climb sugar palms to tap their precious sap. Children carry milk, yogurt or cheese from a goat or cow to sell in the village. Grandmothers sell rugs woven from the jute harvested on a neighbor's farm. Grandfathers help with the groundnut harvest that their daughters take to market.

Dozens of activities make up the economy of the family farm, each producing a stream of income that contributes to what the family consumes and saves. These income streams ebb and flow with planting seasons, annual weather patterns, and the health, gender and number of family members available to work.

The most successful family farms, the resilient farms, are those able to develop and benefit from synergies among the elements of both the agricultural and economic systems. A family might sell most of its fresh groundnut crop to a wholesaler but save a portion to roast and salt, measure into tiny packets and sell as snacks in the local schoolyard. Or, after pruning low-hanging branches from hardwood trees to curb shade on its millet field, a family might sell the branches as fuel to neighbors. To deter insects from its rice crop, the family might refine a potent mixture of home-grown garlic, soap and water and later sell the spray to members of another community. These synergies can be powerful, allowing elements of the agricultural and economic systems to strengthen one another and with time to increase the wealth and resilience of the family and its farm.

A worm turns profits

In rural Ecuador farm families began growing boxes of worms in kitchen scraps and manure. When placed in the soil, these worms improved soil quality and health, ultimately improving crop yields. Once families perfected the practice of 'vermiculture' for their own use, they began growing enough to sell the extra worms to neighboring farmers and communities.

The elements of the economic system

The economy of the family farm embraces infinite activity, part of which produces income and food for the family, and most of which remains unseen. Visible economic activities include the production and sale of farm produce, farm products and the value added to goods through 'value-added processing' and labor. Invisible activities include the quiet workings of worms in the soil, plants converting water and carbon dioxide into grain each night, heat in a compost heap, a cover of pigeon pea plowed into a field and stimulating vital biological work in the soil. These activities are silent producers.

Powered by sun, wind, water and the chemistries of nature, they cost nothing except wisdom and work. Yet they drive the invisible farm – the essential agriculture that makes all that is seen, happen.

Two constructs make up the visible economic system. The first construct is the Core Triangle. It includes the core elements of an income generation activity. The second construct, the Outer Circle, includes those factors which influence the effectiveness of the Core Triangle.

The basic triangle of income generation

The Core Triangle includes the fundamental elements of making and selling a product or providing a service. Each side of the triangle is as important as the other two.

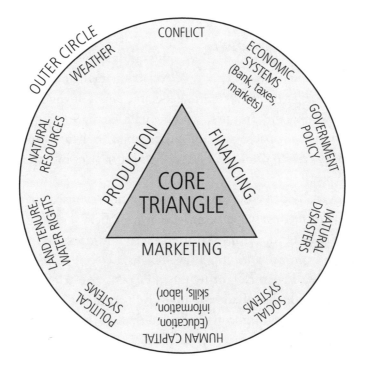

Production: the income generation activity

Crop yields, livestock production, dairy products, fish culture – all contribute to the suite of products, or the product line, of the family farm. Families sell rabbits, weave colorful cloth, or do activities unique to their region. They may collect leaves that fall on the forest floor, stitching and pressing them together to sell as dinner plates. They may collect insects from tuna cactus, convert them into red dye and sell the dye to the local cosmetics company for lipstick.

Families also engage in other forms of income generation besides production, through providing services. They buy charcoal from the farmer near the forest and divide it into smaller amounts to sell to villagers. They purchase clothing from shops that require a bus ride to the border and sell it back to neighbors. These services are also considered part of production.

Nature's own farm

In South Africa some of the poorest farmers do not own land. They 'produce' from the veld. Women gather truffles to sell and herbs for herbal teas. They collect wild vegetables, thatch, fruit and firewood. All activities produce an income.

Producing the product – planting and harvesting the crop, collecting medicinal forest herbs, purchasing sugar to make marmalade and jam – involves costs. So does marketing the product, which includes the costs of storage, transportation, or packaging and processing. Resilient farm families continually seek to diminish these costs to turn sales into the highest possible profit.

There are hidden costs too, costs that do not involve cash, but cost the family nonetheless. Soil nutrients leave a field with the harvest. This is a cost. Future crops will need those nutrients. The rains that water crops can carry topsoil away. This is a cost. Future crops will need that soil. Livestock grazing the same pasture too long can compact and degrade the soil, destroying good pastureland. This is a cost. Future burros, goats and cows will need that pasture. Water pumped into irrigation canals lowers the water table. This is a cost. Future crops will need that water. Pulling children out of school to help with harvesting is a cost that compromises children's futures. These hidden costs are no less important than the out-of-pocket costs that the family must cover to keep the farm healthy and profitable.

Marketing: markets and selling to the markets

Harvested wheat or maize provides value to the family in the form of food, but without a firm appeal to customers, neither has any cash value. The task of the farm is to balance the quality of the crop it has labored to bring to harvest with the costs of producing and bringing it to the customer, a task which requires that the family understand the demand for the crop in relation to similar crops offered by competitors. Without a market – meaning a group of customers – the crop will not convert to cash. Without a good market – a group of customers who will pay the right price – the crop will not convert to profit.

Each major cash crop may have several types of markets. The farm may sell produce directly to customers who consume it. Or they can sell to retail customers, the local stall owners who in turn sell to their own consumers. Or to wholesalers who export to international importers or sell to their own retailers. Each market requires a different approach to pricing, processing, packaging and distribution.

Various farm-based micro-enterprises may have different types of customers as well, each demanding its own marketing approach. These links between farmers, their suppliers (from whom they buy agricultural inputs) and their different customers are called 'market chains'. Market chains are incredibly important and usually poorly understood by development practitioners. Intuitively, farmers understand that there is a market chain, but rarely do they have access to complete information about it, where they as farmers fit into it and how they play a role. This makes it difficult to develop strategies or

Market miracles

In northern Vietnam a family, together with other families in their commune, have two markets for their primary crop of rice.

The family sells rice grain to local stall owners and rice straw to a wholesaling intermediary, distributing it as fodder to retailers in several towns. The family also has two markets for its corn crop, with corn ears sold as animal fodder through a broker and cornstalks sold as fuel to neighbors. From its orchard, the family dries peaches and plums for sale to retailers in the village market.

Each of the rice, corn and dried fruit customers has special needs for pricing, packaging and processing. This farm family tracks the costs and pricing associated with each product and each market to their ultimate benefit.

build strong relationships with others in the market chain. When they are able to coordinate buying and selling, the different people in a market chain can help each other to reduce everyone's costs, while maximizing profits.

Financing: savings and credit

Some activities require only the labor of the farm family to transform a thing of little value (wild grass) into a thing of greater value (a mat or rope). But labor has a cost. The farm family must be healthy to provide the amount of work needed to make such income-generating activities possible. Health requires investment in producing a balanced diet, developing and protecting a clean water supply, constructing a simple home waste management system or purchasing medicine and vaccines.

Most activities also require money beyond any investment in nutrition or health. The family needs money to purchase tillage tools, seeds, a rice mill, tree seedlings and plastic nursery bags, an oil press, bricks for an oven or wood for a potato storage shed. These investments come from savings or from borrowing.

The financing required for an income-generating activity falls into two categories: asset financing and working capital financing. The first, asset financing, occurs when a family buys or builds something that will produce income or reduce costs over many seasons. A chicken coop, a plow,

Politics, schmolitics

Government financing programs for farm families often center on political motives. Subsidized interest rates and forgiveness of debt at first seemed attractive to farmers in Minia, Egypt, a city on the Nile. Later, when these 'services' could no longer be sustained by the government and collapsed, the farm family had to return to the moneylender. This time around the moneylenders, miffed by a gap in business, charged even higher interest rates.

a silo, even a cow are examples. The second category, working capital financing, is when the family uses funds to invest in something that will be transformed into an item for prompt sale. Examples include buying jute to weave into mats, fabric to stitch into clothes or even hiring labor to harvest a tea crop. The resilient farm family knows when and how to balance long-term investment with shorter term working capital.

Most traditional farming communities have various means of developing and managing communal savings, through which farm families save and then borrow. Moneylenders also supplement savings, however their high interest rates deter cost-conscious families. Increasingly, financing is becoming available to farm families through government programs and microfinance institutions.

The outer circle

Shaping the success of the Core Triangle is the economic, social, environmental and political context of the farm. Factors and forces like labor availability, foreign exchange rates, climate patterns and religion and community all have a bearing on the success of the suite of economic activities of a family farm. The following discussion highlights only a few of the most powerful forces.

The competition

Families often farm land with soil, water and climate conditions similar to that of neighboring farms. These conditions limit what the farms can produce, placing them in competition with one another. When many competitors offer similar products to the same group of customers, these customers acquire bargaining power. They can negotiate a low price. Low prices mean slim profits for the farm family.

Resilient farms – with farmers who understand market forces – are able to maintain good prices through a variety of competitive strategies. A family may choose to add value to raw silk by dyeing it. The

Ecuador

colorful thread may suit customers that other farmers do not serve, providing a greater profit for the family.

Another family may segment its apple crop. Instead of selling all the harvest in bulk to a wholesaler who receives a lot of similar produce at the same time of year, the family may select the best apples for packaging to the specifications of a high-end wholesaler and press lower grade apples into juice for sale through other channels. Such competitive strategies require that the family research the variety of available markets, determine the competition for each and decide which market offers the greatest potential for profit.

Community

Farm families rarely work in isolation. When one family needs to terrace a slope, other families will share the work, knowing that next season, they themselves may need to call on neighbors for support.

Farm families not only share labor, they form credit unions, create seed banks and develop agricultural cooperatives. By pooling savings and lending it to farmers, rural credit unions, owned exclusively by farmers in the community, direct cash surpluses to places of cash need. By storing seeds for future planting in small community silos, farmers can

Delayed gratification

Farm families in Nicaragua pooled their resources to purchase a silo. Before purchasing this asset, families were forced to sell their corn at harvest time when prices were lowest. The silo allowed families to store maize until market prices improved, increasing their profits substantially.

separate varieties into different silos and access a greater variety of seed than those produced on their own plots. By developing agricultural cooperatives, families pool their purchasing power for better prices on seeds and fertilizer or equipment. Cooperatives can also attract large wholesale customers who would prefer to deal with one entity over dozens of small farms. By working together, farm families transform competitors into partners.

Synergy and stewardship

The best way to hold costs down and maintain profits is to make the farm efficient. Families that build on the synergies of both agricultural and economic systems are efficient. For example, a family that is already growing neem trees for fuelwood and soap production is efficient when it layers neem leaves in its grain silo to prevent insect damage.

Families that limit waste and use the byproducts of one activity to support another are efficient. For example, a family that converts dirty laundry water into irrigation water for the kitchen vegetable garden is efficient. A family that pens its animals at night on a bed of straw or leaves in order to trap nutritious animal waste, later incorporating the mix into gardens and fields, is efficient.

Families that replenish resources such as soil and water by clever use and management of their labor and natural resources are efficient. For example, a family that terraces sloped fields so that rainwater percolates down into the soil, making it more available for crops and trees on the family's plots, while recharging the local aquifers on which wells depend, is efficient.

Threats to the system

A farm's economic system faces many threats. Natural disasters in the form of fire, hurricanes, droughts, floods and earthquakes may destroy the natural systems on which farms are based, paralyzing the economic systems. Unfair government practices, like unpredictable credit policies, biased land tenure systems or unfair import strategies, can cripple the farm enterprise. So can large farms that decide to compete with the small farm or corporations able to patent specific uses of natural resources on which the family economy depends. Outbreaks of cholera or malaria may weaken farm labor, produc-

Owning nature

The amazing neem tree native to India provides many benefits to the small family farm. It offers valuable shade and firewood, deters pests from grain stores and homes, and contains medicinal oils which can be mixed into soap and toothpaste. Major Indian firms lobbied to obtain patents to any commercial goods produced from neem. Thousands of farming enterprises, that once converted the neem into useful village products, can no longer sell those products legally.

ing a total disruption in the farm's economic system. Plagues of pests may do the same.

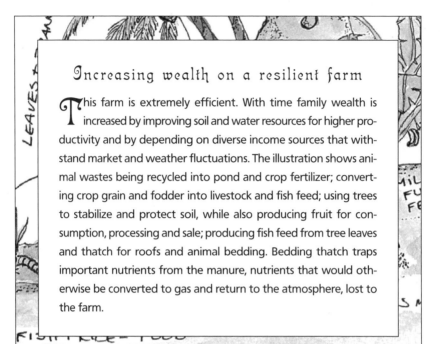

Increasing wealth on a resilient farm

This farm is extremely efficient. With time family wealth is increased by improving soil and water resources for higher productivity and by depending on diverse income sources that withstand market and weather fluctuations. The illustration shows animal wastes being recycled into pond and crop fertilizer; converting crop grain and fodder into livestock and fish feed; using trees to stabilize and protect soil, while also producing fruit for consumption, processing and sale; producing fish feed from tree leaves and thatch for roofs and animal bedding. Bedding thatch traps important nutrients from the manure, nutrients that would otherwise be converted to gas and return to the atmosphere, lost to the farm.

Increasing wealth on a resilient farm

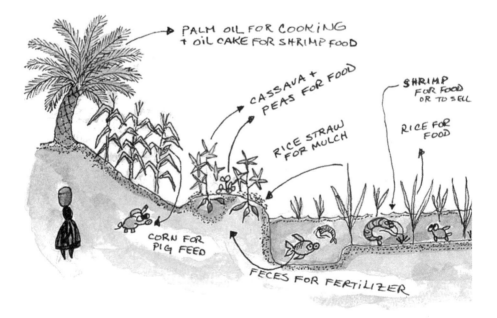

PALM OIL FOR COOKING
+ OIL CAKE FOR SHRIMP FOOD

CASSAVA + PEAS FOR FOOD

SHRIMP FOR FOOD OR TO SELL

RICE STRAW FOR MULCH

RICE FOR FOOD

CORN FOR PIG FEED

FECES FOR FERTILIZER

The flow of farm wealth

With good management, with the fortunes of good weather, access to some natural resources and a favorable socio-economic and political environment, poor farm families accumulate wealth slowly over many years. Their wealth includes natural and man-made assets. It includes the goat pen and the soil, the grain silo and the aquifer. It includes cash, gold and a surplus of favors in the favor bank – the social insurance that ensures good deeds provided to a neighbor can be redeemed in the future. The offering of an ox and plow to the family next door during planting season can be converted into the use of their rice mill after harvest.

A family practicing poor stewardship loses wealth over time. Losses in the form of expenses and hidden costs continue at the same pace while gains remain constant. In contrast, the illustration opposite shows how a resilient farm family increases its wealth over time. Losses are kept to a minimum and a portion of the gains are reinvested into the

farm's ecology and economy. Gains are kept to a maximum by clever management of activities, so that each builds on the other.

Trees on the farm serve as a windbreak for nearby crops, reducing evaporation of precious moisture from crop leaves. Fish eat mosquito larvae and keep malaria under control. Shrimp control pond weeds for greater rice yields. From time to time, the family digs out the bottom of the pond to maintain pond depth and to use as crop and garden soil amendments. Pond silt is composed of eroded topsoil from farm plots, nitrogen-rich fish waste and valuable organic matter from aquatic and terrestrial plants.

Moisture from the pond seeps horizontally into neighboring soils for crops and trees, improving their resilience to droughty spells. Moist soil beneath the pond helps recharge aquifers. Rice straw is used to mulch vegetable gardens conserving moisture and preventing weed growth. It also serves as livestock fodder. This farm family can feed itself a diverse, nutritious diet of dark green cassava leaves, cassava root, grains, fruit, fish, vegetables, animal products, legumes and meat. They earn income from diverse farm products that make it possible to sell throughout the year – surplus crops, crop products, tree products, livestock, fish and shrimp.

We can reduce farm wealth flow to a simple equation – farm wealth at the end of a season equals beginning farm wealth plus the net gain or loss during the season. Included in this accounting are all forms of gain or loss, relative to fluctuations in the value of man-made assets and to the increase or depletion in quantity and quality of natural resources.

Farm wealth flow in one growing season

Final farm wealth	=	Beginning farm wealth	+	Net gain/loss (value of man-made + natural resources)

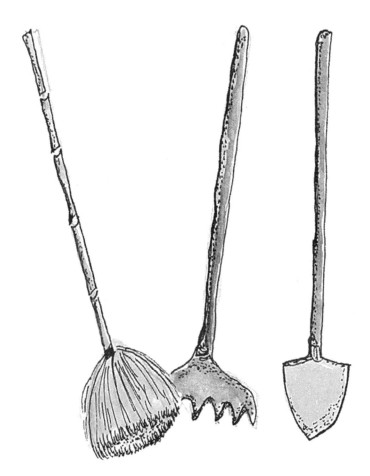

PART II

Supporting the resilient family farm

CHAPTER 5

Resilient farming: approaches to farm family support

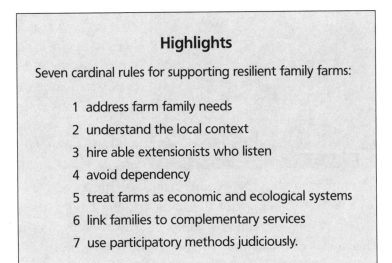

Highlights

Seven cardinal rules for supporting resilient family farms:

1 address farm family needs

2 understand the local context

3 hire able extensionists who listen

4 avoid dependency

5 treat farms as economic and ecological systems

6 link families to complementary services

7 use participatory methods judiciously.

Science and technology

The Green Revolution of the 1960s and 70s promised miracles and delivered miracles. Scientific advances in the form of new seed varieties that responded to synthetic fertilizers were combined with expansion to new agricultural lands. Food production grew to a scale unimagined just years earlier. Plant breeders and agricultural scientists developed high-yielding varieties of basic grains. They developed crop varieties resistant to pests and diseases, as well as varieties that had more protein. They developed crop management formulas designed to maximize yields by applying the right amount of irrigation water and fertilizer at the right time. They tested optimum planting depth, seed and row spacing for 'monocropped' (one crop per field), high-yielding varieties of rice, maize and wheat.

But the Green Revolution had its dark side. Top-down, one way agricultural extension (agricultural advice and support) focused on middle sized and larger farms. So convinced were many experts of science as a panacea that the Green Revolution neglected the adverse effects of science on the environment. New chemicals polluted groundwater, new pesticides killed both harmful and beneficial insects and new cultivation tools degraded soil structure.

Liberia

Perhaps the biggest losers were poor farm families living in marginal environments. Although there were 'massive rises in the yields of staple food crops eaten, grown and worked mainly by poor people,... there [were] only... imperceptible improvements in the lot of the poor'.[1] New technologies 'helped stem the growth of poverty', but did not reverse it.[2] The Green Revolution tended to improve the lives of only those smallholder families who had more equitable access to resources.[3]

In general, the poor lost in four ways. First, population increased and resulted in increasing demand for land for non-agricultural purposes. Additionally, past trends of expansion to new land by larger producers continued during these years and pushed the poorest on to the least suitable, sloped, infertile land. Second, technological advances in the form of tractors, fertilizers, irrigation and weed and pest controls were too expensive for most smallholder farmers. Third, smallholder farmers often got lower yields with 'improved' varieties than with locally adapted traditional varieties. Farmers could not provide the growing conditions required for the new Green Revolution crop strains, and these new varieties were less able to withstand harsher local conditions. Fourth, affordable practices that farmers did try to adopt,

[1] Lipton et al., 1989 in Robert Tripp. 2000. GMOs and NGOs: Biotechnology, the policy process and the presentation of evidence. DFID, ODI: Natural Resource Perspectives, No. 60.

[2] Robert Tripp. 2000. GMOs and NGOs: Biotechnology, the policy process and the presentation of evidence. DFID, ODI: Natural Resource Perspectives, No. 60.

[3] Ibid.

such as monocropping, destroyed the complex lacework of their traditional, more resilient farming systems, leaving family well-being to ride on the success or failure of a single crop.

The Green Revolution was not the revolution of the poor. It was the revolution of scientists and larger farmers, with the benefits of lower food prices going to urban populations. The smallest farm families were left out.

Still, the promise of the Green Revolution and enticing subsidies led many traditional farmers to follow the advice of well-meaning extensionists. They looked to the quick fixes of science and technology that had helped their larger neighbors. Diverse cropping patterns, resulting in stable production, often disappeared in favor of monocropped fields, with farms producing a single cash crop. If cash or subsidized inputs were available, traditional manures were replaced by purchased fertilizers. Local pest and weed controls succumbed to chemical pesticides and herbicides. Plowing by animal traction gave way to tractors. The result? Often a few years of surplus, followed by deficit, at the expense of modest, but stable production.

Farmers discovered that abandoning traditional systems during the Green Revolution could be expensive, inappropriate and sometimes harmful. Soils loaded with chemicals washed downstream and polluted

Liberia

75

Double-edged sword

Modern technology was never so eagerly adopted as it was in the breadbasket of India, the state of Punjab. Improved crop varieties, tractors, irrigation and agro-chemicals helped India double grain yields during the Green Revolution. The state of Punjab now pays a high cost for this modern-day production miracle.

1   Increased irrigation has depleted groundwater, and now only the better-off farmers can afford to dig deeper wells and buy the larger pumps that farming now requires.

2   Standing water from irrigation systems is causing increased rates of malaria.

3   Tractors have compacted soil so severely that 'hardpan' layers at 23–31 cm (9–12 inches) prevent roots from getting water and nutrients from deeper in the soil. This means farmers have to apply extra fertilizer at greater cost to maintain yields.

4   Extra fertilizer pollutes drinking water supplies with carcinogenic nitrites and nitrates.

5   In fields where monocropped wheat and rice are planted in rotation year after year, pests and disease are flourishing. Additional pesticide use has increased harmful residues on harvested crops.

6   Overproduction has led to lower prices and surpluses.

7   Increased costs for tractors, equipment and agro-chemical inputs combined with lower grain prices have meant small or no profits for farmers.

8   Finally, counterproductive government trade policy has worsened an already difficult situation.

– Reijntjes, Coen, Bertus Haverkort and Ann Waters-Bayer. 1992. *Farming for the Future*, London; MacMillan Education Ltd., p.7.

the waters of lowland farms and villages. Pests and weeds developed chemical resistance, becoming super-pests and super-weeds. Careless irrigation left soils too salty for crops. Single crop farms could not withstand a disease outbreak or a price drop in the marketplace. Modern equipment was expensive, inappropriate for use on sloped land and created compact soil layers, degrading soil structure over time.

Yet farmers, researchers and development workers learned from these mistakes. They now know that what works is to combine many elements of traditional farming methods with appropriate elements of modern production techniques and good market strategies. Balancing the old with the new in wise ways can move a farm family from subsistence into prosperity, and does so without impinging upon neighbors or damaging a farm's chance to provide for generations to come. When farms are able to achieve this fine balance, we call them *resilient farms*.

Some cardinal rules

Because resilient family farming is the result of blending the best of traditional farming methods with selected new technologies, the effective development practitioner must understand the local context for farm activities. This context includes traditional methods for carrying out activities, farm family priorities and the multiple, different seasonal demands on the farm family. The practitioner must also understand which new methods in technology, processing, financial services or marketing are appropriate for farm families. To help practitioners transform the smallest family farms into resilient farms, we offer seven 'cardinal rules' as guidance.

Address the needs of the farm family

Green Revolution practitioners focused on two things – the production side of agriculture and farm men, ignoring other important activities in the agricultural cycle – processing farm produce, preparing it for the table and marketing farm goods – activities often in the domain of farm women. Practitioners also ignored the role of young adults, children and members of the extended family.

In recent years, increases in the number of rural men migrating for day labor wages, often over long distances, have imposed new stresses on the farm household. Women find themselves managing more than

The resilient farm

The graphic on the facing page illustrates the idea that balancing production and natural resource conservation with income generation is essential to the resilient farm. The best rural development projects support all three goals.

Lower left: When production, resource conservation and income generation are all low, farms cannot support farm families. Projects with poor results for all three factors should be abandoned or redesigned.

Upper left: Farms or development projects that focus only on production that protects the environment may be fine for meeting subsistence needs, but undermine the farm family's ability to earn income and use it to access healthcare, pay tuition, buy farm inputs, invest in assets and increase options.

Lower right: Farm families who ignore resource conservation and focus mainly on production to generate income can cause adverse environmental impact and compromise subsequent production and children's futures.

Upper right: Farms and projects that balance all three factors – production, conservation and income generation – are more likely to provide both food and income today and tomorrow. These farms are high return conservation farms, or resilient farms.

their children, doing more than processing farm produce or marketing goods. Women are running the farm.

In countries with high rates of HIV/AIDS, productive adults are disappearing in large numbers. Grandparents and the eldest child are actually running the farm, if there is any farm left to run after selling farm assets of livestock and land to cope with the negative economic impact of AIDS.

The resilient farm

THE RESILIENT FARM
[HIGH RETURN CONSERVATION
FARMING]

INCREASING ABILITY TO CONSERVE FARM RESOURCES

INCREASING RETURNS FROM CROP + LIVESTOCK PRODUCTION

Families valued

In Kenya, a development organization taught local communities how to conduct their own problem assessments and prescribe their own solutions. The whole family contributes to each problem assessment. The community talks to every man, woman and child, engaging them in a variety of activities before offering assistance. Communities now manage their own agricultural extension and financial services, calling on experts when needed.

Modern development practitioners now acknowledge the family unit as a source of labor. They understand the many priorities, demands, risks and stresses placed on the family and on different members of the family.

They also understand the critical social and economic ties between family, neighbor and community and the increasing role of women in managing the totality of household affairs.

Do your homework

Before designing an irrigation system, promoting a community grain processing shed or advising a village on the purchase of a tractor,

understand the community's priorities, their traditional methods of farming and their typical activities. Understand how a new irrigation system or equipment will affect other members of the watershed. Water trapped at the top of the watershed may improve the supply for families in that community while reducing the supply for farms below. Tractors plowing local fields may compact the soil, hasten water runoff and increase soil erosion so that downslope families find their own supply filled with sediment.

Debtors prison

A well-meaning development agency advised a community of farmers in the highlands of Central America to construct an irrigation system. The system required transporting water over 11 kilometers. The cost of construction materials was high, so the agency financed materials for the irrigation system with loans to participating families, only to cripple them with debt afterwards. One family had to sell its land to make good on the loan. Clearly, the agency had not helped analyze the scheme's costs in relation to its benefits, nor had it looked at a role for subsidy.

Employ humble, but alert extensionists

Poor farm families are risk-averse. Harsh and unpredictable conditions can threaten survival each year and wipe out family reserves. No matter how enthusiastic extensionists are when promoting an 'improved' planting practice or new livestock vaccine, farmers usually analyze the risk–benefit ratio for themselves. If the risk seems unacceptable, they ignore the extensionist entirely, or they allocate only a small corner of their plots to testing the new method. Some let more daring farmers test the new practice, while cautious families wait and watch.

Once proven locally, useful innovations spread like wildfire from farmer to farmer, without formal extension services. (It should be noted that during the Green Revolution subsidies and donations of improved seed and agro-chemical inputs changed the risk–benefit ratio so that, temporarily at least, farmers were more willing to follow locally untested extension advice.)

Avoid dependency

In the past, development agencies provided technical advice about mechanized agriculture to male farmers, often accompanied by gifts of improved seed varieties, livestock breeds, tractors or agro-chemicals. Small farmers often became dependent on external sources for farm inputs. When the inputs vanished, so could the farm.

To avoid dependency, the prudent development worker needs to be a partner, planning projects based on the needs of the farm family, on awareness and assessment of environmental impacts, on risk analysis and information sharing. Activities that support independence and local control include:

Working ourselves out of a job

High on the slopes of the Andes in one very remote area, no local organizations are in place to bring essential services to farm families. An international acency hired a team of local staff including a medical doctor, a nurse, a forester, an agronomist and an agricultural extensionist to provide needed services through a small project. After five years, the agency, in keeping with its mission to strengthen local capacity, is supporting this team as they form a new local organization that will provide quality services permanently to other communities in the area.

- participatory training and judicious technical support
- locally run credit services
- capacity building for community organizations and local farm cooperatives
- marketing support.

Treat farming as an economic and ecological system

No matter how isolated or how poor, most rural farm families are linked in some way to market economies. Affected by crop prices, weather patterns, international commodity markets and shifts in labor and consumption, these families are part of a globalized world.

To survive within an economy in constant flux, the farm family needs information – data about crop prices, short and long-term weather forecasts, improved breeds of livestock and improved management practices. It also needs economic resources such as credit, savings and insurance. Learning how to coordinate with other producers, input suppliers and wholesalers can lead to resilient farmers who capture profitable market niches.

Similarly, in some areas, conserving essential natural resources is almost impossible. Natural resource degradation can be so severe that it reaches a point of no return. Long-term, unchecked deforestation can lead to complete loss of topsoil on sloped lands, making farming extremely difficult (for example, in parts of Central America, India, Congo, Indonesia, Bolivia, Haiti, Brazil). Deserts can spread when poor irrigation management leaves soil so saline that crops will no longer grow (Pakistan, India, West Africa). Trapped aquifers can be pumped dry (West Africa, India, Pakistan) so that there is no water left for irrigation and no possibility of recharge.

Over-irrigation of aquifers depletes fresh water, so that ocean salt water can intrude on farmland, killing trees and other vegetation and destroying coastal farmland (Gambia, Thailand, Bangladesh). Or an entire region can have such low groundwater levels that groundwater irrigation disappears as an option. When combined with thin topsoil, low groundwater levels in semi-arid or arid climates make agriculture extremely difficult (sub-Saharan Africa). Deforestation and lost habitats mean losses in biodiversity, sometimes irrevocably (Brazil, Indonesia, Philippines, Haiti, Sudan).

In such cases, simple resource *conservation* is not enough and must be replaced by resource *rehabilitation*. Yet resource rehabilitation can be too costly for rural farm communities. So initially, national or international agencies may need to bridge the gap with subsidy. For

Farming for the future

In Africa, a PVO gathered 25 agronomists from its programs around the world to develop guiding principles for all the agency's agriculture programs.

The main tenets they developed instruct development workers to practice conservation farming (agriculture which preserves and restores natural resources), to advise farmers in high-yielding, low-cost production methods that bring profits and are also environmentally sound, and to work within the context of a watershed, considering the impact of activities in one area on farmers, villagers and the environment in other areas.

These principles now guide staff and projects to improve agricultural production of the poorest farm families while conserving valuable natural resources, meeting today's needs without compromising tomorrow's harvests.

Saltwater intrusion, The Gambia

the poorest farm families, rehabilitation must also be linked to immediate production benefits. Families may also need training in new ways to use, rebuild and recycle farm resources efficiently, without polluting or degrading. They may need to develop an awareness of habitat –biodiversity relationships or learn how to re-establish local habitats.

Link families to a complement of interventions

A child becomes ill and needs health services. A husband wants to terrace a slope and needs construction advice from an expert or the help of neighbors. A farmwife wants to build a new goat pen so the child who takes them to pasture each day can go to school. This justifies a small loan for wood and wire. A farmer needs to add harvest weights from a scale, but cannot read or write. This requires schooling.

Cambodia

The wide range of needs on the family farm means no single intervention will be of much use over time. Only different interventions – extension, credit, insurance, education, healthcare – provided in a coordinated way and driven by farm family demand, will satisfy different needs over the course of seasons and the life of the family farm.

Development programs can no longer work in the cocoon of their various sectors or separate areas of expertise. Nor can they operate on the principle that what development organizations have to offer is what farmers must accept. Demand must drive development services.

Financial services programs know that a physically strong and healthy farm family improves the chances of a loan being repaid. Agriculture extension programs know that without savings or credit services, the farm will not have the resources to expand and make wise investments. The agriculture program's success will improve if it links the farm to good financial resources and encourages the farmer to link to profitable markets.

Health programs know that good nutrition is critical to good health and that the farm must produce enough food and a balanced diet or earn enough money to supplement farm production with nutritious purchased food. The health program would do well to link the farm to good agricultural extension services for production of nutrient-rich grains and vegetables. Health, agriculture and microfinance programs all have more enduring impact when linked to adult literacy programs that target reading lessons to instruction on healthy diets, improved crop management for higher yields or more accurate record keeping for village banking projects. For these reasons, development practitioners in any one sector can increase impact when they link families to technical support in other sectors.

Practice participatory methods with care

Since the late 1980s, rural development organizations have adopted a variety of techniques to engage villages and farmers in the design, management and evaluation of programs. These techniques provide invaluable information about the village – its geography, resources, history, threats, economic activities, seasonal patterns and the relative wealth of its members. Because of these participatory exercises, development programs have enjoyed better results in delivering services prioritized by communities.

Burn-out

In Nepal, a study showed that communities are disgruntled about dozens of development organizations taking days of their time asking the same questions. Some have taken to posting Participatory Rural Appraisal results on a water tank, asking any new development workers to refrain from additional information-gathering. Said one community member: 'We have done this already, go get the information from the water tank.'

However, participatory methods can backfire, causing negative reactions in rural communities. Intense participation pulls community members away from their many demands, requiring them to meet with development workers for long hours, drawing maps and seasonal calendars, discussing the relative poverty or wealth of neighbors or identifying major cultural events and days of social importance. This time spent is costly to the community.

Adding to this burden are different development organizations (or even different programs within one organization) each assessing a community without coordinating results.

As development practitioners, we really must take an honest and critical look at the reasons we are using participatory approaches. Participation does not occur when we push for community consensus for our initiatives, nor when we 'mobilize' the community to 'volunteer' to participate in our activities, projects and programs.

Haiti

Wise development workers will respect the time that participatory exercises require and limit participation to what is essential. Here are a few tips:

Participatory principles

- Avoid duplication; work with other organizations to share results and investigate project and community histories.

- Understand the periods in the year when time is scarce; refrain from participatory exercises at that time.

- Schedule community interviews in advance so the community can allocate time.

- Give communities the option of not participating in participatory exercises.

- Do not make receipt of service to an individual family contingent on participation in the assessment. (At a community level, refusal to participate may indicate project burnout or lack of interest in the project. Listen to verbal cues. Look for non-verbal cues.)

- Start any process with a brief participatory analysis or reflection, so that the community can dictate its own priorities for information and initial project activities.

- As community priorities evolve, additional participatory decision making can take place gradually.

- Ensure that development staff truly grasp the principles and philosophy upon which participatory methods are based. Avoid using any methods which project staff apply automatically without understanding why and to what end they are being used.

- Be aware that marginalized members of a community (women, youths, the elderly, ethnic minorities) tend to remain silent in large group meetings, yet often have divergent views that are critical to project success.

- Realize that participatory appraisals raise community expectations of receiving assistance.

The seven cardinal rules in this chapter are not the only cardinal rules, but they reflect critical lessons from the field. They are based on successes, failures, mistakes and observations. They can set the stage for more effective collaboration and support of farm families.

Take home message

Farmers and development practitioners both bring something to the table. Learn from and work with each other to meet a range of economic, social and ecological needs.

Liberia

CHAPTER 6

The ripple effect: agricultural extension services

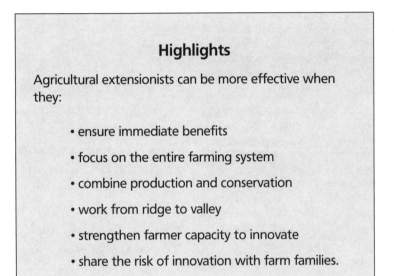

Highlights

Agricultural extensionists can be more effective when they:

- ensure immediate benefits
- focus on the entire farming system
- combine production and conservation
- work from ridge to valley
- strengthen farmer capacity to innovate
- share the risk of innovation with farm families.

Spreading success

The best way to support poor rural communities is through sharing information and providing skill training. This transfer of knowledge from trained agronomists to farmers is called 'agricultural extension'.

Today's development agencies promote 'participatory extension' in which information transfer is a two-way exchange. They also promote 'sustainable agriculture', or environmentally sound production.

Unless new to farming or new to the area where they are farming, rural farmers know their environments, needs and priorities. They know what traditional farming methods and systems have worked well in their climates, soils and environments in the past. Agricultural extensionists generally do not have this information.

Agricultural extensionists, working hand in hand with scientists, microfinance and business development specialists, know which newer production technologies are most likely to enhance local practices, which product quality strategies will satisfy urban markets and which financial services are likely to serve the family best. Farmers generally do not have this information.

Out of the woods

Pushed from their forests by national law, groups of illiterate, lower caste, migratory forest dwellers who survived outside the cash economy in India find survival difficult. Their forest survival skills are now worthless, and they lack even the most basic skills for farming, their main alternative.

Development agencies are working with these tribes to teach the basic elements of literacy and farming — sustainable, low cost practices, like tillage, planting, weeding, composting and gravity-fed small-scale irrigation. Adults have now made a successful transition to a new way of life, growing enough food to feed their families.

The best extensionists work closely with farmers to prioritize locally appropriate interventions, deciding what will yield the greatest short-term and long term benefit for the least labor and cost and deciding which alternatives to test in local environments. Extensionists create a ripple effect of success by spreading information about appropriate advances, trends and technologies. Farmers create a ripple effect of success by sharing their own innovations with extensionists and other farmers.

Some cardinal rules

The poorest farm families tend to farm the smallest plots on the worst land. They fight for survival in the most undependable climates, the harshest socio-political environments and the most fragile natural environments. Any agency that intends to support these families needs to follow some basic guidelines.

Guarantee immediate benefits

Farm families struggling to survive do not have the luxury of participating in projects with only long-term benefits. Projects must also put food on the table and money in pockets today.

When development agencies promote projects that are long term, such as reforestation or terracing for soil and water conservation, farmers tend to go along with the projects as long as the projects provide food-aid incentives, compensate for manual labor or subsidize the cost of materials. As soon as the project is over, or as soon as an economic crisis occurs, the family is apt to harvest the project trees for quick cash or neglect them due to competing demands on their time.

The best extensionists look for activities that combine three goals – short-term gains, long-term benefits and rehabilitation of natural resources. Any project that can answer yes to the following questions passes the litmus test for this cardinal rule.

Crop of rocks

Working through many development organizations, an international donor funded the reforestation of Haiti's deforested mountains with millions of trees. Today, none of these trees remains. Because of successive political and economic shocks, poor farm families were forced to cut the trees to sell as lumber and firewood in order to survive during each new crisis.

Had the donor and development agencies included in their projects schemes to generate instant, ongoing benefits, farmers would not have been forced to resort to leveling the new forests. Now, instead of a crop of hardwoods, these mountains grow bare subsoil and rocks.

1 Will this project increase production and income within three to six months?
2 Will this project rehabilitate the natural resource base?
3 Will the fruits of this project still benefit the farm family 10–20 years from now?

Strengthen farming systems

Traditional farmers think of their farms holistically, as complex systems requiring elaborate multi-tasking to manage multiple cycles, products and relationships. No one element is seen in isolation from any other. All activities are linked and interdependent. The more complex the farming system, the more stable and resilient it is likely to be, the more nutritious the family diet and the more secure the family's income.

If drought or disease ruins the rice crop, deep-rooted, drought-resistant fruit trees and fish ponds will still produce. Rich silt from the bottom of fish ponds can be used to fertilize fruit trees. Farmers feed rice

Growing a pension

Agronomist and author Roland Bunch (*Two Ears of Corn*) developed a no-till agroforestry production system with Honduran farmers, combining practices from the Sahel and Central America. Farmers plant slow-growing, high value hardwood trees 7–8 meters apart. In the open spaces, velvet bean (*Mucuna deeringiana*) is planted between rows of maize.

When left to grow and re-seed itself year after year, *Mucuna* rebuilds degraded soils in extraordinary ways. It improves soil fertility, adding high amounts of nitrogen; prevents erosion; helps soil retain water; outcompetes weeds and speeds creation of new topsoil. *Mucuna* also increases corn yields. As part of the dispersed tree system, *Mucuna* gives farmers strong disincentives to the generally destructive slash and burn clearing.

When a 50–50 maize–*Mucuna* mash is prepared and fed to pigs, farmers enjoy an immediate triple gain:

1   Pigs mature faster on this protein-rich diet, increasing efficiency of production and translating into higher profits in less time.

2   Field corn, generally a commodity with low profit margins, is transformed into high value pork.

3   In approximately 15–25 years, this system provides the farm family with high value mahogany, cedar or teak for sale.

straw and high-protein leaves from trees like *Leucaena* and *Acacia* to fatten fish and livestock. Livestock produces manure that improves soil fertility, and fertile soils grow high-value vegetables for sale, as well as maize for livestock feed and family meals.

Starting where farmers are, endorsing the wisdom of the ages and complementing the traditional with appropriate modern advances, extensionists can increase the probability of improving food security and decreasing rural–urban migration.

The 49–51 rule, or balancing production with conservation

The minute that human beings decide to clear land and till the soil, they initiate a process of soil degradation. While we may have the legal right to till the soil we own, we also have an ethical responsibility to future generations to replace what we take.

'Sustainable agriculture' was coined as a response to the failures of the Green Revolution, years before it became popular to talk about 'sustainable projects'. In the development world, sustainable projects are understood to be those in which activities or benefits continue long after the development agency has packed its bags and moved to another community. In agriculture, 'sustainable' refers to production practices which mimic ecosystem processes and balance resource extraction with replenishment. Sustainable agriculture incorporates efficient recycling of resources like water and soil nutrients, and depends on complexity and diversity to strengthen the entire farming system.

Since poor farm communities are often located on the most degraded land, production combined with conservation is unlikely to reverse negative environmental trends.

The 49-51 rule: During the time that an agency works directly with a community, up to 49% of the agency's efforts and resources can be focused on triage – resolving immediate, short-term problems and production issues. But at least 51% of project efforts must focus on long-term, system-wide goals and objectives. These might include rehabilitating natural resources by replanting perennial vegetative cover at forest or farm plot margins, supporting development of permanent financial services, subsidizing community construction of a potable water system or promoting a community health center that farm families support.

Work from ridge to valley

When agencies work in rural areas, they begin with one set of communities, phasing out the old and phasing in the new over time. For agencies targeting the poorest, the higher, remoter areas of watersheds tend to be the areas where the poorest farm, so it makes sense to locate projects there initially. From the perspective of natural resources management, starting at the top of the watershed also

Sesame Street

In the 1980s and 1990s an international agency promoted West African export production of high quality sesame seeds for tens of thousands of women farmers. Often the land allocated by village elders to women for growing sesame was already degraded. This land was poorly farmed for many years and considered barren by villagers.

Sesame produced well at first, because it is hardy and tolerates infertile soils. After several years on the same plot, sesame could no longer grow because the unfertilized crop had extracted the last remaining soil nutrients. The development agency had focused on increasing yields and ignored proven soil replenishing techniques.

Now, in some areas, villagers call sesame the crop that ruins the soil and creates desert.

Sustainable hillside agriculture

CONTOURS WITH TREES
AND GRASSES PREVENTS
EROSION AND RUNOFF,
CONSERVING
PRECIOUS TOP SOIL.

Sustainable hillside agriculture

Farm families in the watershed shown on the previous two pages are combining production and conservation. They plant live barriers of thick grasses, hedges and trees on the contour of slopes to prevent erosion and runoff, conserving precious water and topsoil to increase and maintain good yields. They plant diverse annuals (vegetables, legumes, tubers and grains), perennials (fruit trees, fuelwood and lumber trees) and raise livestock and fish to ensure a varied, balanced diet and a variety of products for the market.

Families recycle animal wastes to fertilize gardens and fish ponds, use crop grains and stalks for animal feed, grow hardy cassava on higher and less fertile soils, grow cut-and-carry alfalfa on slopes near the sheep pen and leave hardwood trees at the top of the watershed to protect sources of water.

helps to focus on critical forest cover, which protects vital water sources and prevents erosion that will fill lower rivers and reservoirs with sediment. Working from ridge to valley generally makes both social and ecological sense.

Develop farmer scientists

For every approximately 1,000 soil scientists working in temperate zones, there is only one tropical soil scientist focusing on tropical agriculture. In addition to fewer public sector scientists supporting agriculture in the tropics, agriculture ministries and national research institutes in developing countries tend to be underfunded, understaffed, focused on medium and larger-scale farmers or completely defunct.

This is a problem because agriculture is site-specific. The perfect solution in one area can be the worst solution in another. The ideal rice variety for one region hardly germinates in another. Every technique and innovation needs local testing and refinement before widescale promotion.

What does this mean for development practitioners? It means we need to seek tools, methods and manuals that show how to simplify and adapt scientific plot trial and data analysis methods. Include the farm family wherever possible in simple, straightforward research, design and testing of agricultural methods and innovations. Families will supplement the extension worker's suggestions and experience with practical knowledge of traditional farming methods that work locally. The contributions of both groups diminish risk in a new project and allow the best chance of success.

Share the risk

How many agricultural extensionists in how many countries have academic degrees in fisheries, economics, biology, social work or philosophy with little or no on-farm experience, providing only book-learned technical advice to farmers? How many agronomists with formal academic training in methods for large scale, commercial agriculture provide advice and subsidies that sway a community to monocrop one high-value, high-risk cash crop? The crop earns high prices today and terrible prices tomorrow, as neighboring communities copy success and flood the market. How many agricultural extensionists who do in fact have vital farming experience with smallholder plots have advised farmers to take risks that they themselves would not?

Walk in the farmer's shoes. Promote only what is sure to be a success. Find ways to share the risk.

Oops

In one part of Guatemala, where sloped soils are sandy and provide good water infiltration, extension workers instructed farmers to dig ditches to improve water infiltration, believing it would decrease run-off and increase crop yields. So, the farmers dug the infiltration ditches. When the rains came and pounded the sandy soil, the ditches collapsed. 'I have had to redig this ditch 100 times,' complained one farmer. 'The only reason I do it is to qualify for my family's food rations.'

These extension workers only had experience working in another part of the country, where the clay soils really did need improved water infiltration and the ditches held up well during rainstorms. Clearly, these extensionists did not understand that different soils require different interventions, nor had they tested the new intervention in the new location first.

- Pay for market studies.
- Do careful cost–benefit analyses. Define costs and benefits broadly – labor costs and demands, environmental impacts, changes in family roles and relationships.
- Provide thorough, ongoing technical advice for new methods of livestock production or crop management.
- Cover the costs of expert consultants to design and supervise construction of small-scale irrigation systems or any other new production systems.

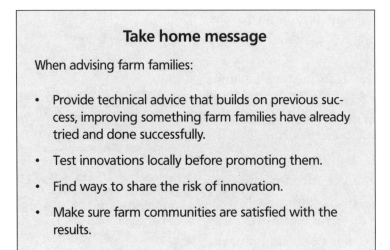

Take home message

When advising farm families:

- Provide technical advice that builds on previous success, improving something farm families have already tried and done successfully.

- Test innovations locally before promoting them.

- Find ways to share the risk of innovation.

- Make sure farm communities are satisfied with the results.

El Salvador

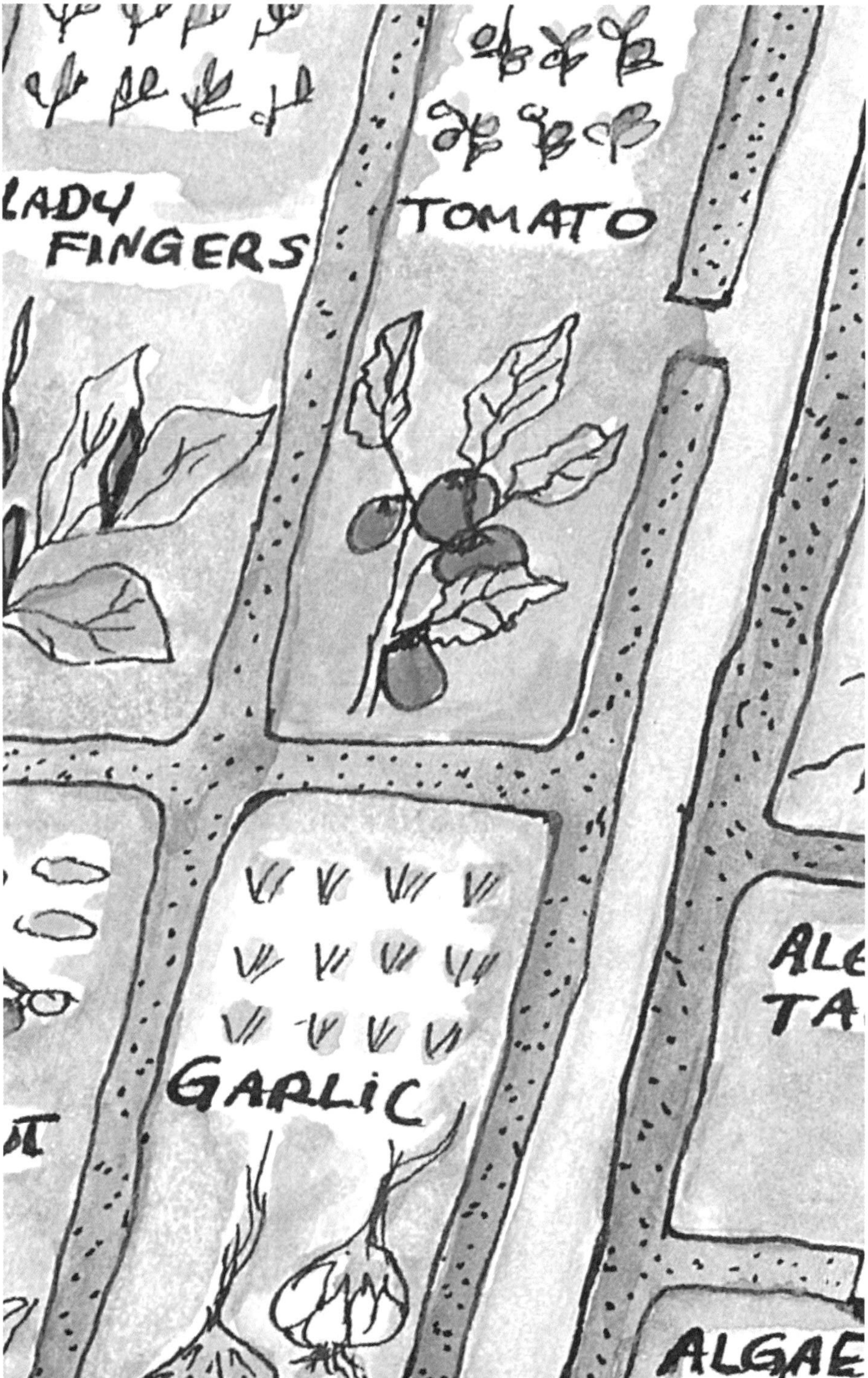
LADY
FINGERS
TOMATO
GARLIC
ALGAE

CHAPTER 7

Barn-raising: support for building farm assets

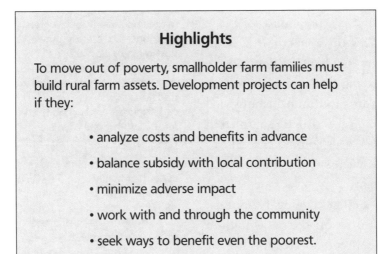

Highlights

To move out of poverty, smallholder farm families must build rural farm assets. Development projects can help if they:

- analyze costs and benefits in advance

- balance subsidy with local contribution

- minimize adverse impact

- work with and through the community

- seek ways to benefit even the poorest.

The dilemma

In the 1960s and 1970s, organizations dedicated to improving tropical agriculture invested large sums of money and countless hours boring wells, building large dams, constructing large, elaborate irrigation systems and buying tractors. When development workers completed their work, they left the community. After their departure, farmers returned to traditional ways of farming. They left reservoirs to fill with debris, breed disease-carrying insects and eventually collapse. They let tractors idle and rust for lack of parts. They let ditches gather leaves and soil, until they could no longer serve their intended purpose.

What went wrong? Farm families had not chosen these activities nor had they contributed to them – not with their money, not with their labor. Free services were assumed to continue without end. Why should the family toil to maintain a water pump when the nice development workers who constructed it might someday return for repairs?

What can be done?

Most cultures maintain traditions that reflect the community spirit of 'barn-raising'. Members of a community gather to build a barn, a church, a schoolhouse, or create terraces on a neighbor's land. 'Many hands make light work,' the saying goes, and it is true. Not only does communal labor speed the time needed to complete a project, it also promotes a sense of pride and ownership in work well done.

Whether digging fishponds, or infiltration ditches, building chicken coops, greenhouses or goat pens, the development worker must honor the traditions of cultures where work is shared and collaborative results appreciated.

Missing the forest for the trees

An international agency worked with local Guatemalans to improve soil and water conservation in maize and bean fields. 'Farmers' contributed to terracing their sloped maize plots only half-heartedly. When the project was over, 'farmers' returned to their traditional work – judiciously cutting forest hardwoods to craft furniture, while the hillside conservation systems deteriorated.

Had the development workers done their homework, they would have supported the community's economic backbone – its beautiful carpentry, not the small maize-bean plots that the carpenters maintained only to meet minimum subsistence needs for their families.

Some cardinal rules

Analyze costs and benefits

Building infrastructure to improve farm life involves many costs. There are the costs of building the bridge, the drainage system or the road. And, there are the costs of maintaining the system once it is built. For example, when analyzing the costs of building a small-scale irrigation system, the family or community must calculate how much of its available funds are invested in an asset like an electric pump and how much is depreciated over time versus how much is needed to cover recurring costs of maintaining the pump. The family farm must understand the social costs and benefits as well and try to place a value on them.

Balance subsidy with local contribution

The wise development worker optimizes the impact of subsidy: too much subsidy and the community has nothing at stake, so the project fizzles when the development worker leaves. Too little subsidy and the community may not be able to afford the project at all. Wise use of subsidy includes subsidizing materials for initial construction or providing pro bono advice by a consultant for designing the project. Unwise subsidy includes funding the cost of on-going maintenance and repair.

All for one

In Liberia, a local NGO assisted poor farming communities to rehabilitate and convert their low-lands for rice production. Working with the community, the NGO provided technical advice on leveling gently sloped land and forming dikes around the new paddies.

Local farm families were accustomed to working in groups for labor-heavy tasks and appreciated the fact that the NGO collaborated with community members to design the project, thus ensuring community ownership, tapping community work crews for the heavy, but necessary labor investment and strengthening local expertise for future maintenance.

South Africa

Biogas farm assets

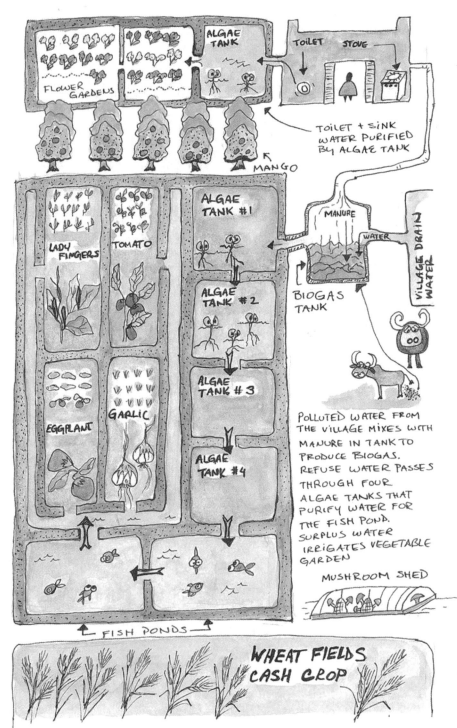

FLOWER GARDENS

ALGAE TANK

TOILET

STOVE

← MANGO

TOILET + SINK WATER PURIFIED BY ALGAE TANK

LADY FINGERS

TOMATO

ALGAE TANK #1

MANURE

WATER

VILLAGE DRAIN WATER

ALGAE TANK #2

BIOGAS TANK

EGGPLANT

GARLIC

ALGAE TANK #3

POLLUTED WATER FROM THE VILLAGE MIXES WITH MANURE IN TANK TO PRODUCE BIOGAS. REFUSE WATER PASSES THROUGH FOUR ALGAE TANKS THAT PURIFY WATER FOR THE FISH POND. SURPLUS WATER IRRIGATES VEGETABLE GARDEN

ALGAE TANK #4

MUSHROOM SHED

← FISH PONDS →

WHEAT FIELDS CASH CROP

Biogas farm assets

Over a five-year period this farm family increased its assets using project microfinance loans to build one biogas and five algae tanks. Neighbors pitched in to dig the huge pit for the biogas tank.

The biogas tank produces gas for the family stove and heats the kitchen in cold weather. The family purifies gray water from the nearby village in the algae tanks and then uses it for fish ponds and gardens.

The family has paid back the loans with the increased income that now supplements their modest traditional wheat profits. They sell to a lucrative cut-flower market in the city and to a fish middleman. The grandmother sells surplus vegetables in the local market. Mushrooms are dried and sold directly to a soup factory in the city.

Minimize negative impact

Trapping water upstream may affect a community living downstream. Installing a silo to store dry season fodder for goats, but not a pen to restrain them during the rainy season is folly. Animals will roam unrestricted, destroying neighbors' crops and overgrazing the land. The development worker must avoid planning for one family in isolation from neighboring families. Developing strategies to respond to possible effects of the project on surrounding land in the watershed

Men at work

In Ethiopia, an international agency invested in new roads so that coffee farmers could move their produce to market. To ensure that the poorest received benefits, the agency offered rural workers food and a stipend in exchange for their roadwork. When the roads were finished, so were the stipends. These workers then returned at the end of the harvest to resume their coffee-picking jobs, only to find that they had been replaced by other laborers. Had agency staff analyzed the possible negative impacts of the project, they would have designed one that took into account the farming seasons.

will lessen negative impact on the natural environment and preserve good relations among farm families.

Build on community organizations

Most communities have various organizations, however informal, to help manage community activities. Members of these organizations know the lives of community members and how each family earns its living. They know health status, seasonal habits, religion and often family needs. These organizations also understand community priorities – when to build a school, repair the village water pump, construct a storage shed for the farmers' cooperative or repair a church or temple. Most importantly, these organizations have the ability to gather community members when it is time to enlist their support.

Engage these organizations in project design and to facilitate planning for maintenance and repair. Ensure that they understand and agree to the long-term responsibilities of maintaining the outputs of a project. Together with local leaders, community members oversee fee collection for water use, run the local credit cooperative, manage a community seedbank or take up a collection to assist a family in crisis.

Pay it forward

Working closely with a community organization in Ecuador, development workers helped plan a small-scale irrigation system. The community agreed to charge reasonable fees for water use. 25% was allotted to maintaining the system, 50% to increasing capital in their community bank and 25% to high priority activities that would benefit even the poorest families.

So far, this project has earned enough money to pay for a visiting nurse, cover part of the salary of the local schoolteacher and subsidize the cost of veterinary medicines and vaccines.

Include a social aspect

Development workers often support a project with a social agenda in mind, to improve community healthcare for all or improve access to potable water. Enlist the support of community organizations to prioritize a socially beneficial component, particularly one that includes the poorest community members, often those who are landless with the least means to earn a living.

Take home message

Keep infrastructure development small and straightforward so that families and communities can take part in design decisions, play a major role in construction and take responsibility for maintenance and repair of their new assets.

Vietnam

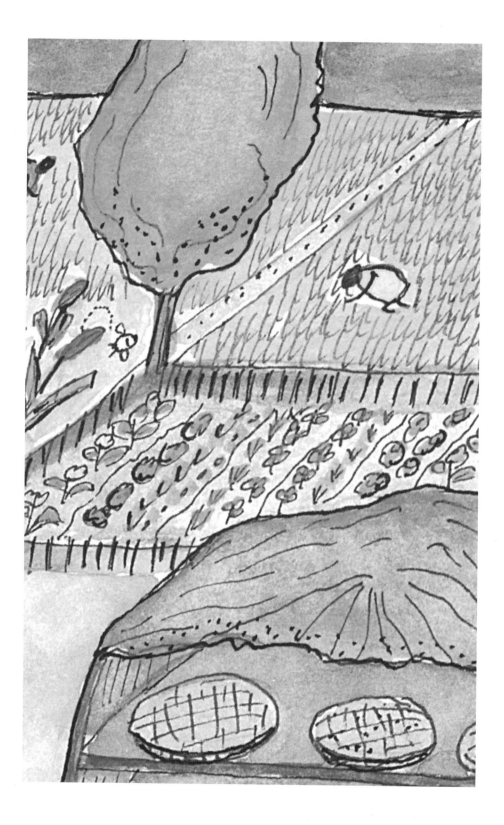

CHAPTER 8

Inspiring growth: developing farm enterprises

Highlights

Resilient farms are successful at both farm production and income generation. Development projects can support farm enterprises best when they:

- identify family priorities

- know the market

- ask the right questions

- build on family experience

- encourage substitution

- add value to products

- turn problems into opportunities

- encourage diversity.

The dilemma

The woman rises well before dawn. So does her husband. It is harvest time, and every available hour is used to gather and thresh grain from the fields. After harvest, the family stores and sells the grain. And then they wait. They have some grain and cash from the harvest but it runs out well before the next planting. The husband leaves to find work as a day laborer far away. The woman is left behind with her children. They spend most of their time gathering wild yams and berries in the woods or sleeping to conserve energy.

What can be done?

In contrast to the preceding scenario, the family on a resilient farm

Waste not, want not

Mindanão, Philippines. While fishermen are busy catching and selling fish, a local farm woman comes to the shore each day to gather the remainder of their catch – shells, coral and small sea creatures caught in the nets. She polishes the shells and coral and dries the tiny seahorses to export to Manila. This activity sustains her through the off season of her rice crop.

sees every waking moment as an opportunity to improve their assets or income. They use the dry season to plant tomatoes and onions in kitchen gardens irrigated with discarded gray water from the household. They raise rabbits or collect fallen branches from aromatic trees bordering their grain plots. They collect eggs to sell or gather wild nuts. They make tomato chutney, carvings from colorful wood, beeswax candles and incense from aromatic wood pulp.

There are other ways to increase income on a family farm. The family can open a tea kiosk or start a small vegetable stand. Or make sweets from their fruit trees and peddle them to schoolchildren. Or tap and boil sap from sugar palms to sell in the city. Added together, these many small activities allow the family to sustain itself over the seasons.

Development workers, as part of a 'business development service' agenda, are often eager to support the family in undertaking new activities. However, they usually provide advice that asks the family to try completely new activities, such as raising a dairy cow, pounding leather into shoes or sewing intricate designs on cloth.

These ideas are risky for three reasons. First, the family may not know how to do the activity. And in order to learn the new activity, time consuming and expensive training is often necessary. Even if training is successfully completed, talent for a particular business, especially one that requires artisanal skills, cannot be 'taught'. Second, the family may not want to do the activity. Third, the activity may create dependency, moving the family away from traditional work that sustains them into new work not yet proven as viable. Finally, the size of the market – a group of customers willing to pay the right price – may not justify the new activity. In all these instances, the project is likely to fail.

To support the farm enterprise, development workers must under-stand the triangle of income generation (called the Core Triangle in Part I). A critical side of the triangle is the base, or the market. The market – a group of customers – is often the last thing a self-employed farm family wants to build. But it is often the single most important element.

THE MARKET

The market – a group of customers who will pay the right price for goods and services.

Financing – credit and savings.

Production – agricultural products, goods and services, such as harvested crops and meat, crafts, tea stalls, manure for city gardens, processed foods.

Some cardinal rules

Development workers intent on supporting the farm family in its business activities will do well to follow a few simple rules.

Identify the family's priorities

Ask the family what activities it sees as priorities and opportunities. A business activity chosen by the family is far more likely to get full commitment than one suggested by an adviser or extension worker. Refrain from advising families on what their priorities ought to be.

Know the market

Before the family engages in a new activity or expands an existing one, the family must determine if it can sell the new product or service at a good price. This means family members must talk to potential customers and understand their needs. (See Chapter 9: Going to Market.)

Families must also determine if other people in the market chain – like middlemen – will promote or limit the family's ability to get a fair market price for their goods. The family must talk to other producers to gather this information.

Ask the right questions

Development workers do not need to know all the answers. They need to know how to ask good questions. Sometimes simple stories illustrating how a farm has grown over time followed by a few good questions can provoke discussion and useful answers from the farm family. Or drawings showing a good enterprise and a poorly performing one can stimulate discussion about the farmer's own performance. By not giving advice and by asking the right questions, development workers can coax the best ideas and solutions from farm families themselves.

Build on what the family knows

Chances are family members have a variety of skills already: baking snacks, weaving rope, raising fowl. Instead of embarking on an enterprise that is foreign to the family, discuss possibilities that build on the family's strengths. Can snacks be sold in town? Can the rope be woven into a hammock? Can four chickens become twenty? By expanding what the family already knows how to do, its members gradually become used to larger endeavors. At some point the family may feel ready to transform 20 free range chickens into a chicken coop of 100 chickens, producing eggs for market and bagged chicken manure for city gardeners.

Families able to substitute a 'product bought' with a 'product sold' turn expenses into profits. By converting funds spent on on-going purchases to funds invested in economic activities, the family enjoys a double gain – reducing on-going costs while increasing income.

For example, if a family purchases silk yarn to weave into fabric, they might consider growing mulberry trees around the edges of the farm and cultivating 'silk worms' in small sheds. They can sell the raw silk yarn to manufacturers and keep some for their own dyeing and weaving. If the family does not have the space to perform all these tasks, they might divide the various steps of the process among neighbors, each earning a profit.

Reap what you sew

In a rural community in Zimbabwe, farming women, weakened by HIV/AIDS, found they could not afford to purchase school uniforms for their children. Using loans from a local organization, they purchased sewing machines and fabric.

The crisp new uniforms worn by their children soon attracted compliments from neighboring communities. Now, these women have a profitable business that makes and sells school uniforms throughout the province and serves as a training center for their daughters.

Add value

At times, farm families overlook activities that spring naturally from primary activities. For example, if the family is harvesting groundnuts on one plot of the family farm and a neighbor is producing charcoal on her small forest plot, some of the charcoal might be purchased to roast the groundnuts. If roasted groundnuts fetch a good price, then the farm may profit. It may profit far more than if it sold only raw groundnuts.

Turn problems into opportunities

Do marketing bottlenecks prevent the production or sale of goods? If so, the enterprising family can remove these bottlenecks so that all in

Sericulture on a resilient farm

115

the community benefit. For example, upon examination of the market chain for chickens, a family discovers that all local poultry producers have difficulty finding low-cost, high-quality chicken feed. Making and selling chicken feed could be a service where everyone wins. The chicken producers have a new supply of feed, and the farm family earns more revenue producing feed than selling chickens in a saturated market.

Encourage diversity

Ecological systems are stronger and more able to weather threats when they hold many different life forms. This same principle is true for economies, large and small. The economies of entire cities have collapsed when their enterprises were geared to one industry. Conversely, economies that include a variety of industries tend to nurture businesses that feed off one another, so that collectively these enterprises have both local and external markets.

The economy of the family

The sea around them

In a coastal village in the Dominican Republic, farmers grow cassava, sorghum, maize, tobacco and pigeon pea. Because rains are scarce, yields are insufficient to sustain a family throughout the year. After harvest, men take to the sea to spearfish and to the forest to hunt game. Women gather wild medicinal herbs to sell for healing purposes. When the sea turns turbulent from seasonal rains and prevents spearfishing, it's time to plant the fields. In a harsh environment, these farm families cope through diverse, but complementary, activities.

farm is no different. Varied economic activities allow the family to cultivate several markets for different products. If one market temporarily lacks purchasing power, another may enjoy robust demand. Similarly, if one crop fails, another activity may prove healthy and continue to provide income to the family. Diverse activities also allow the farm family to take advantage of labor surpluses at different times of the year.

Avoid group activities

More often than not, when a group activity is related to income generation, it fails – whether it is cooperative candlemaking or a community butchery.

Bottomed out

In Thailand, a well-meaning development organization encouraged farmers to raise pigs collectively. The families took out a loan and bought piglets to fatten. When the animals matured, pigs from neighboring China flooded the market and depressed prices. To repay their loans, families sold their pigs at a loss.

If a group spends much of its labor cultivating mushrooms, and the price of mushrooms falls, then the village economy feels the impact. If a disease wipes out the community goat cooperative, then the whole community suffers.

Screen for yield

Development workers often fall into the trap of promoting unprofitable businesses. Producing crafts for specialty markets is a ubiquitous favorite of naive organizations. But craft production rarely generates profits for the farm family and robs family members of precious labor.

Encourage families to make goods for local markets where risk is minimal. Advise them to include their labor when assessing profitability of economic activities.

Take home message

Build on strengths

The farm family is in the best position to choose its activities.

They know what they want to do and what their strengths are.

Encourage them to build on what already exists before leaping into new ventures.

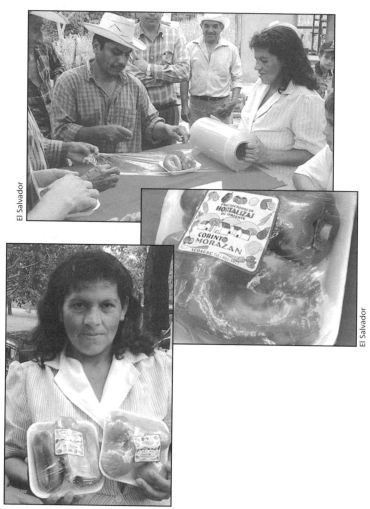

El Salvador

El Salvador

El Salvador

CHAPTER 9

Going to market: support in selling farm products

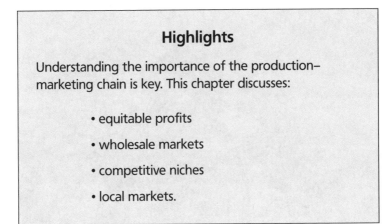

Highlights

Understanding the importance of the production–marketing chain is key. This chapter discusses:

- equitable profits
- wholesale markets
- competitive niches
- local markets.

The production–marketing chain

PRODUCTION⇨PROCESSING⇨PACKAGING⇨WHOLESALING⇨RETAILING

STORAGE AND TRANSPORTATION

The dilemma

Getting the farmer's harvest into the hands of those who will consume it asks the farm family to understand the various steps their product must take on its journey to the customer. This journey, often seen as puzzling or unimportant, is called the production–marketing chain. Most families would prefer to produce goods, and leave the work of selling to happen by itself. But with no customers,

Diverse products for diverse customers and multiple markets

PALMS PRODUCE OIL, THATCH AND WOOD. COCONUTS, AFTER EXTRACTING MILK AND MEAT, CAN BE SOLD AS COW FODDER.

SOME VARIETIES PRODUCE SAP TO BE BOILED INTO SUGAR

CASSAVA

COMPOST

FISH POND PRODUCES PROTEIN YEAR-ROUND

products stay on the farm with little hope of taking the journey that will produce income for the family.

Some farm enterprises may have a simpler chain, yet it is a chain nonetheless. Selling honey or tomatoes may require little more than the farmwife gathering her products in the morning and selling them a few hours later to a stall owner in a local trading center. She must treat this production–marketing chain with the same care as she does the more sophisticated system that brings her primary cash crops to market. She must understand the needs of the family purchasing her

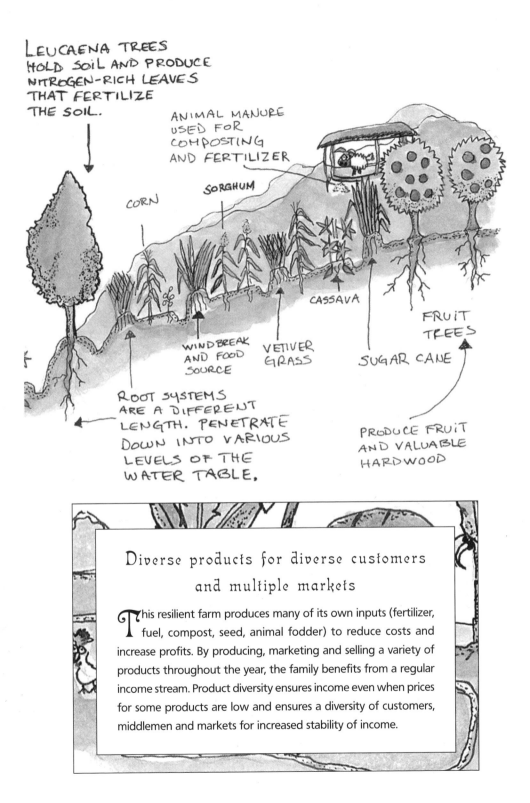

LEUCAENA TREES HOLD SOIL AND PRODUCE NITROGEN-RICH LEAVES THAT FERTILIZE THE SOIL.

ANIMAL MANURE USED FOR COMPOSTING AND FERTILIZER

CORN

SORGHUM

CASSAVA

FRUIT TREES

WINDBREAK AND FOOD SOURCE

VETIVER GRASS

SUGAR CANE

ROOT SYSTEMS ARE A DIFFERENT LENGTH. PENETRATE DOWN INTO VARIOUS LEVELS OF THE WATER TABLE.

PRODUCE FRUIT AND VALUABLE HARDWOOD

Diverse products for diverse customers and multiple markets

This resilient farm produces many of its own inputs (fertilizer, fuel, compost, seed, animal fodder) to reduce costs and increase profits. By producing, marketing and selling a variety of products throughout the year, the family benefits from a regular income stream. Product diversity ensures income even when prices for some products are low and ensures a diversity of customers, middlemen and markets for increased stability of income.

honey and tomatoes, so she can prepare and package them accordingly. She must also understand the needs of the stall owner. The stall owner may want fruit graded or honey in jars or insist on making purchases only in the morning. If she understands her customers well, she can even begin to grow new varieties of produce or create new products to meet their needs.

Some cardinal rules

Ensure each participant in the chain makes a profit

If the activities of any participant in the chain are not profitable, then the chain collapses – the weak link theory in action. Subsidized entities, such as development organizations, should not participate in the chain, unless:

- they limit their role to advising, facilitating linkages or educating producers, customers, donors and governments
- there is a permanent subsidy available to guarantee their place in the chain
- they serve in a temporary capacity with a profitable replacement already in mind.

Non-profit organizations run the risk of creating dependency – other participants in the chain grow to depend on their services – without assuring their own permanence in the chain. For example, many well-meaning organizations have tried to take on the role of middleman to help farmers bring their products to market. These efforts are often subsidized and when funds vanish, the project ends and the farmers

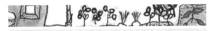

are left without important middleman services. Better strategies involve working with the community to:

- identify strong local middlemen and teach farmers how to negotiate the best deal
- invest both money and training in trustworthy local entrepreneurs who are interested in starting a responsible middleman business (for a profit)
- assist farmers in identifying

where in the production–marketing chain they have the best comparative advantage. For example, if they want to break into the chain that sells milk or butter to cities and the farmers already grow maize, they may wish, as an entry point, to provide maize and husks as feed and fodder to those who own the dairy cows

- link farmers to government services, if available and if dependable
- as a last resort, help farmers create their own middleman services in the form of a new organization. This organization must be able to recover its costs completely beyond any initial subsidy needed to launch it.

Take advantage of the wholesale market

What are the needs of a woman, for example, who buys mangoes

Patient profit

In Nicaragua, an organization worked with a local middleman to assist farmers. The middleman researched the market and found that if farmers in his community waited a few months after the harvest, they could sell their maize for more in local markets. He was glad to store and distribute the maize for a reasonable fee.

There was also a positive byproduct of meeting with neighboring farmers – the middleman grew to understand the families and believed it was in his best interest to give his own community a better deal.

in the local market? What kind of packaging does she like? What quality is she willing to pay for?

The farmer's goal is to maximize profit. If the farmer knows that the end customer, the woman buying mangoes in the market, would like attractive packaging and a colorful, firm, juicy mango and is willing to pay more for that mango, the truly resilient farmer chooses the best marketing channels to get her what she wants.[1]

By understanding the customer, the farm family can add value to their products and sell additional products with lower marketing costs. Getting a brand new customer is extremely expensive. Keeping that customer and selling her more products is a way to build on the initial marketing expense. Once farm families understand each member of the production–marketing chain, the family can look for new ways to please customers – new varieties of produce to grow, new products to make on the farm and new ways to package products to increase sales.

The market rules

In Burkina Faso, the wife of a farmer sells tomatoes in the local market. While competitors in the market pay top dollar to buy the graded produce they then sell, this woman knows her customers and how they use her products.

She grades the tomatoes herself, placing over-ripe fruit for cooking in one bin, firm fruit for salads in another, and semi-ripe fruit for eating later in the week in yet another. Housewives are able to choose the fruit they need.

This farmwife passes on some of her savings to customers in the form of lower prices and keeps some for herself in the form of profits.

Orient the farm family to their competitive niche

Who is the competition? Who is selling high quality cabbage and where? Do competitors sell just one crop or provide wholesalers with a variety of produce and farm products? What are competitors charging and how does their product quality or their pricing compare to that of the farm family? When the farm family understands its competitors, it can better determine strategies for production and marketing.

The family will also better understand its competitive advantage and strengthen that advantage to increase sales. For example, if the family

---

[1] Although farmers often sell directly to the end customer, they also sell to wholesalers who buy larger quantities and provide faster turnaround with less time and expense for the farmer.

learns that competitors supply wholesalers with large quantities of a single grain at harvest time, then the family may wish to invest in a silo to store the grain, so they can supply the wholesaler later when he is low on grain.

Understanding the market and the competition helps farm families develop a pricing structure that earns a profit. Naturally, the family must understand its costs, including the cost of production, preparing the product for market through grading, packaging and processing, as well as the costs of transporting and storing the product.

The 60% threshold

Markets remote from the farming source represent risk. The more distant the market, the less the family understands it and can control it. To keep risk to a minimum, encourage families to produce goods where 60% of sales come from local markets. In this way, the farm family can observe market behavior and respond as behavior changes.

Bowled over

A tribal family in eastern India gathers leaves from Sal trees in the forest to press into leaf plates. The plates, sold in town, hold food at wedding feasts and other celebrations. Leaf pressing requires a special machine and mold. The family came to realize they were barely earning a profit – many people in neighboring communities produced the same goods, flooding the market.

The family took it upon itself to travel to town to learn what else retailers sold along with the leaf plates. Their answer? Leaf bowls. They discovered retailers were always short of bowls. The family borrowed money for a new mold and began producing bowls, earning more because there was greater demand for this 'product extension.'

Take home message

Know the market before producing

The farm family must understand each participant in the production–marketing chain before it can match the product or market strategy to client needs and preferences. The marketplace also includes competition, and the farm family must understand where its goods and services stand in relation to the competition.

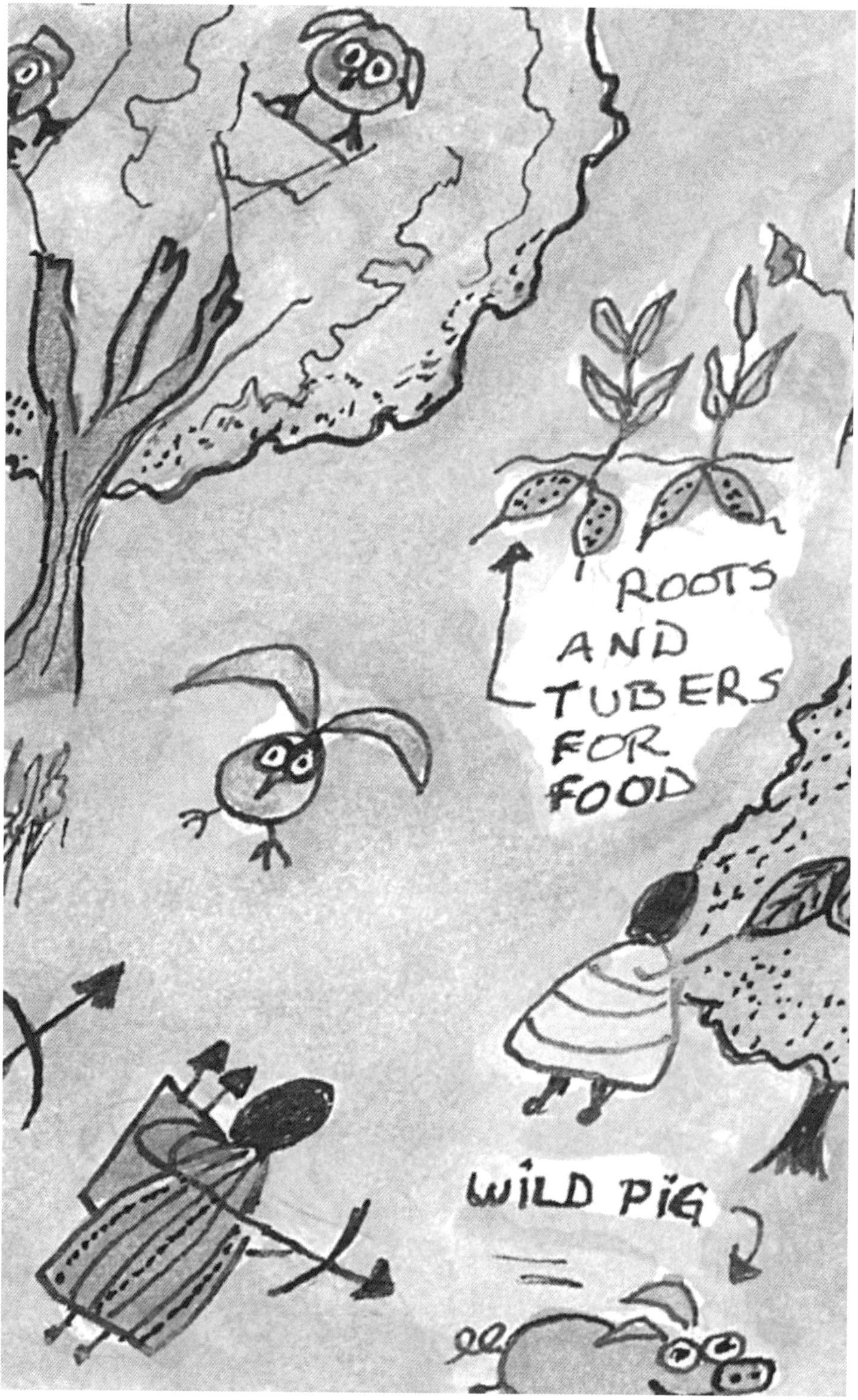
ROOTS AND TUBERS FOR FOOD
WILD PIG

CHAPTER 10

Banking on the family: financial services to farm families

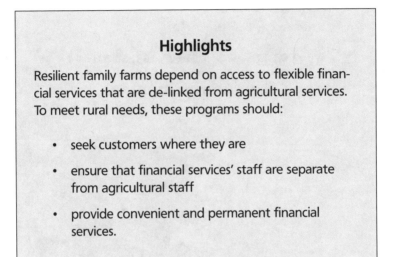

Highlights

Resilient family farms depend on access to flexible financial services that are de-linked from agricultural services. To meet rural needs, these programs should:

- seek customers where they are

- ensure that financial services' staff are separate from agricultural staff

- provide convenient and permanent financial services.

The dilemma

The smallest of smallholder farm families use cash to manage activities. They invest cash in grain silos, water-harvesting systems and animal pens. They spend cash on school fees, medicine and clothes. Their cash comes from sales of agricultural produce and farm products, from savings and credit or from renting out the family plow.

To pay for medicine, a festival or a burial, the farm family often finds itself in the position of having to sell an entire animal or a whole tree when only some of the cash generated by the animal or the tree is needed. The rest may go to waste. Most families would like to use credit or savings services to manage their wealth better.

In recent years, many agricultural organizations have started financial service programs that offer credit and savings to support small farmers. Nearly all have failed. They fall short of properly serving the farm family or sustaining their own operations beyond a few seasons.

What accounts for such failure? These initiatives are not managed as professional services, but rather as adjuncts to agricultural programs. Typically, programs tie credit and savings to specific agricultural projects, not to the priorities of the family. When the time comes to repay loans, families resent not being able to choose the loan's use. If

The forest as an extension of the family farm

FLOWERS FROM THE MOHUA TREE FOR ALCOHOL

LEAF PRESS FOR LEAF PLATES

LEAVES FOR ROLLING CIGARETTES

FODDER

the high-yielding hybrid crop failed or the piglet died, they refuse to repay the loan.

Another reason that credit activities inspired by agricultural projects fail is that these projects mix staff responsibilities – one day staff are supportive and advise farmers about seed varieties, the next they collect late loan payments. This conflicting set of goals and activities damages the relationship between staff and farmer. It also leaves managers

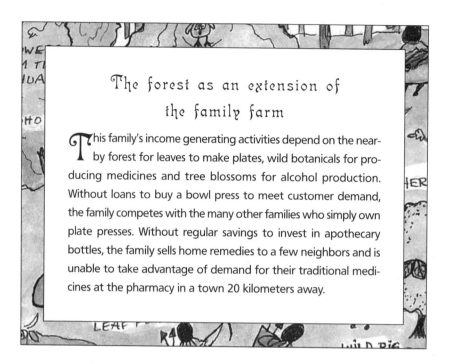

The forest as an extension of the family farm

This family's income generating activities depend on the nearby forest for leaves to make plates, wild botanicals for producing medicines and tree blossoms for alcohol production. Without loans to buy a bowl press to meet customer demand, the family competes with the many other families who simply own plate presses. Without regular savings to invest in apothecary bottles, the family sells home remedies to a few neighbors and is unable to take advantage of demand for their traditional medicines at the pharmacy in a town 20 kilometers away.

at a loss as to how to motivate staff to accomplish very different tasks with very different objectives. The result? Dissatisfied farmers, discouraged development workers, dismal loan repayments and zero sustainability.

Perhaps the greatest failure of these programs is their 'project' orientation. They ignore the long-term commitment implied in the provision of financial services. Agricultural loan programs tend to offer credit that is a one-shot deal – credit linked to livestock introduction, credit linked to a disease-resistant crop, credit linked to constructing a small-scale irrigation system. Like most families, farm families require a mix of credit and savings services throughout the farm's life – a loan for ducks in one season, a loan for a well in the next, and in the next, a loan for a new variety of melon seed or fabric to stitch into clothes.

Where agricultural initiatives have failed to manage finance programs successfully, microfinance institutions have failed to provide services to suit farm families. These institutions have developed one or two products, often very rigid, to which families must mold their needs and behavior. This is an unrealistic request, and one that runs counter to modern business practices of good marketing and customer service.

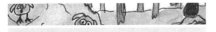

Reeling it in

In Eastern Thailand, where the rains produce only one rice crop each year, villages are very poor. A local organization offered savings and credit services to farm families. One family already grew mulberry trees and invested loans in simple sheds where they practiced sericulture – the production of silk from silk worms. After the caterpillars created a cocoon of fibers, this family would reel the fibers into silk yarn.

The wife found the reeling process caused serious elbow pain. Her husband crafted a special reel from local materials. Not only did the wife's pain vanish, but she found she could reel more efficiently. When neighbors asked for similar equipment, the family invested its next loan into manufacturing the new machines. Now the eldest son is able to earn a living by making and selling this simple equipment.

Microfinance programs have focused on their own institutional viability, presuming that an institution sustaining itself implies a rural customer base also sustaining itself. This assumption appears to work in the short term, when new customers continually flow into a program, replacing dissatisfied ones who leave. Stability of the institution is only a mirage, because in fact the institution is weak.

Over the long term, a revolving door of customers points to a lack of suitable services. This exodus of customers is causing some progressive microfinance programs to realize that their long-term viability depends on how well the institution serves and retains customers. When customers do well by the services of the institution, customers are loyal to that institution and both customer and institution prosper.

What can be done?

When properly managed, financial service programs supply a continuous stream of support to farm families. If the development organization believes the farmers in an agriculture project might need quality financial services, it should begin by talking to the men and women in farm families to answer the following questions:

Speeding ahead?

In Cambodia a development organization has learned that lending to local businesses located in a rural area forces the lender to understand the economic ties between farm and non-farm business activities. For example, local 'moto' repair shops complain they can't pay back their loans when the harvest is poor or global markets for rice are down. Why? Farm families don't have sufficient income to pay for moto maintenance.

- What are the farm family's financial service needs? For what purposes do farmers need to save or borrow?
- Where or how are families currently meeting their needs, if at all? Do these services meet all or some of their needs?
- Are there formal services available, for example through a rural bank or a specialized microfinance institution? If so, what is the quality of these services? Will they meet family needs? If not, is the institution interested in tapping into this new market? Is it willing to develop products and services that suit these families?
- If not, are there other informal savings and credit services that farmers may access such as local, traditional savings and credit groups? Will these services address family needs? If so, link families to them.
- If the farming community has no resources appropriate to its situation, the development organization might develop a financial services program.

Some cardinal rules

Go to the customer

Farm families are busy managing their farm, their enterprises and their household activities. They do not have time to travel long distances to receive financial services or to  attend multiple meetings. Some programs make regular rounds to individual farms to collect savings. Others frequently send a credit officer to the village to meet with loan groups to issue loans and collect payments.

Guard against risk

A financial services program cannot sustain itself over time if it offers risky loans.

Five ways to guard against risk

1 **Start small.** Like any skill, managing debt takes time to acquire. Start families with very small loans, as little as $5 to $50 so that they get used to making steady repayments. As their capacity to manage credit and their business activity increases, they can borrow larger amounts. Small loans are low risk to both the family and the lending institution.

2 **Use social guarantees.** Group guarantees are an excellent way for families new to borrowing to develop credit discipline and a credit history. The best guarantee is a good credit history and a good relationship with the program.

3 **Match payments to household cashflow.** Loans become risky when payment times and amounts do not coincide with the cash flow of farm families. If cash flow varies, consider making the repayment variable. Work out the schedule in advance with the farm family based on cashflow of the household. Include all household cash in the analysis, not just the activity intended for a loan.

4 But...**require mininum monthly payments.** Though payment amounts may vary, always require some payment, even if it is interest only, at least once a month. For long-term loans such as those designated for pig-raising or growing hardwood trees, ensure the farmer has the cash in the short term to make minimum payments. Part of the loan might be used to plant beans, raise fish or weave shawls – activities which generate cash quickly.

5 **Finance what the farm family knows and what it wants.** Development practitioners find it tempting to suggest the family invest in certain new, high investment activities such as goat-breeding or raising exotic fruits and vegetables for export. This often leads to disaster, causing high risk to the lender and to the family. Only finance the priorities of the family and what members already know through experience or solid training. Never advise on loan use.

Provide convenient, flexible services

Borrowing needs vary for the farm family, depending on the season and the intended activity. No family uses loans for identical purposes time after time. Some require loans for a crop in one season and savings for food or emergency in the next. Good programs create highly flexible products based on loan use and the family's ability to repay. Useful savings services support the family's variable cash flow. Farm families, often illiterate, appreciate convenient, low hassle procedures with few or no forms to complete and two-day turnaround times between loan application and loan receipt. They also appreciate easy access to savings.

Specialize staff

From the inception of a financial services program, a multi-purpose development agency must ensure that the financial services component has well-trained staff dedicated to providing financial services. Mixing duties prevents staff from developing a strong learning curve and enjoying a logical career path.

Mixing duties also confuses farmers. One day a field worker comes to give production advice and another day, the same field worker comes to pressure the farmer on a late loan payment. Switching from friend to foe can frustrate both parties.

Plan for permanence

A family will use financial services repeatedly if services are good. Farm families grow to depend on them in the same positive way that large commercial entities depend on their banks. A financial services program has an obligation to become a permanent resource for farm families.

There are two routes to permanence. The first route involves situations where farming communities and the farms themselves are disperse, remote and distant from good roads. In this instance, the development organization may wish to establish permanence through locally managed, community-owned financial associations. Savings and credit groups, self-help groups and local associations are a few of the names given to these grassroots clusters. Yet they are essentially the same – staff mobilize between 20 and 70 families who save regularly and disperse savings to those families in need of loans. Groups follow a democratic process for deciding who receives a loan and the length of the loan term.

The development agency's role in this case is to help organize and train these groups so that they may sustain themselves over time, even when the development agency ceases its support. Sustainability at the grassroots level calls for these groups to be able to perform simple bookkeeping procedures and charge an interest rate that covers losses, the hidden costs of inflation and a return to savers. Most groups charge between 2 and 7% interest per month. Interest stays within the group fund.

The second route to permanence involves situations where the population is less sparse and the development agency believes a sufficiently large customer base will support institutional sustainability. In order to provide quality services over the long term, a high-performing institution must price services so that interest and fees cover ongoing expenses. Initially, when the program is small, it lacks sufficient income to cover costs. Cost coverage can be attained when the program reaches 5,000 families. If a new institution is called for, good customer service, disciplined financial management and sound institutional planning pave the road to permanence.

Take home message

Serve the customer

Both agricultural development programs and microfinance institutions have served farm families poorly. However, if programs listen to the customer, they can provide permanent, flexible resources that suit the farm family for many years.

Specialize

Focus the financial services program on providing just financial services. Allow staff to become expert at their jobs of promoting quality financial services to clients.

Choose the right route to permanence

Farm families want financial support throughout the life of the farm. To continue providing needed services, development organizations must create local associations or professional financial institutions.

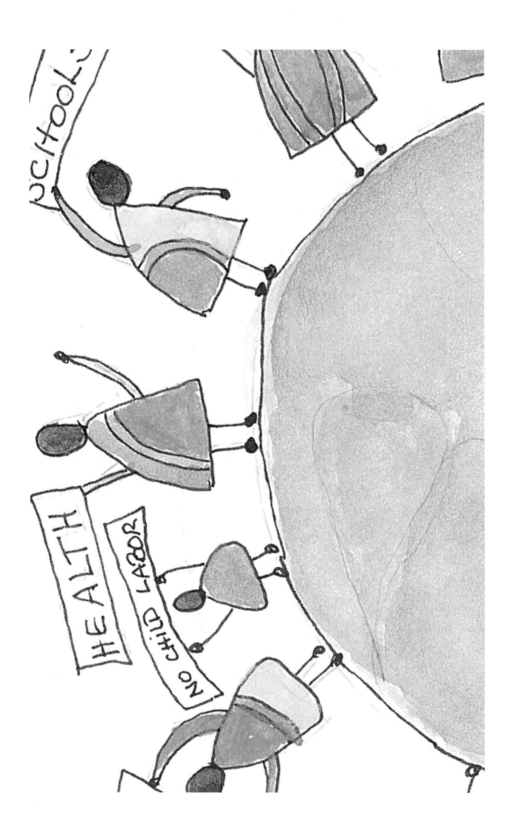

CHAPTER 11

Speaking truth to power: advocacy for the family farm

Highlights

Global, regional and national trends and policies can have greater impact on farm household outcomes than activities occurring within farm borders. To support farm-friendly policy, NGOs and PVOs can play an effective role in advocacy that:

- avoids placing farm families at greater risk

- is simple

- links to professional advocacy organizations

- is based on critical analysis of macro-level trends and transnational issues.

The dilemma

The family farm may take its crop to market one day, sell a few chickens the next week, bring woven mats to the wholesaler on the next and still find that it is no further ahead in income or assets than the year before.

The village gossip brings news that the government is flooding the market with rice at harvest time. Or the tax collector comes demanding his due. A state official threatens to push the family off land it has owned for generations, yet to which it holds no legal title. The local credit agent claims no more credit is coming the farm's way – the government has placed a cap on interest rates so that the bank cannot cover its costs, forcing it to close the door to the family farm. Even the most artful managers of the family farm face ruin from the effects of unsupportive government policy.

For decades, agricultural support focused on science, improved technologies and training. While these efforts produced advances, they did not address the powerful forces of government policy, policy that can support the farm or destroy it.

Government subsidies and pricing policies can tamp down any chance for prosperity on the small family farm. Policies can change food storage and consumption patterns, encouraging farmers to sell all their stored harvest when prices are high, only to spend limited cash later to purchase food. Taxes and business registration requirements appropriate for larger businesses can be cumbersome for micro-enterprises such as local street vending and small trading activities, leaving many to operate these enterprises illegally or to close them.

Unfair policies are one problem. Unfair services are another. Many government programs offering agricultural services have ignored the poor or advised them to farm in ways that place them at risk. These services often focus on advice and support that is more appropriate to larger farms, putting the small farm family in the position of having to change their patterns to conform. If they do not conform, they receive no benefits at all.

For example, small farms seeking credit often find themselves forced to borrow large amounts

Good deeds

In Ecuador, as in many places, the poorest farm families often lack formal legal title to land they have owned for generations, placing their homes and assets at risk. The development project linked rural farm families to local lawyers who volunteered their time to walk villagers through government procedures to title their land. Now 1,700 indigenous families in one area of the mountains have legal title to their land, making their futures more secure.

Ghost schools

With funding from a major international entity, the government of one country launched a program to benefit the rural poor, creating thousands of primary schools across the country. Large landholders gave permission to house the schools on their land, neglecting to give road access. Today, farm children cannot get to these 'ghost schools' nor can teachers. Instead, the structures house livestock for the landholders. Appropriate advocacy might have prevented the problem.

for major cash crop production to take advantage of the only government credit available. Sometimes smallholders change from production of several crops, livestock and coffee trees, for example, to production of one crop in order to generate a yield large enough to warrant credit. This shift disrupts the fragile lacework of the diverse smallholder farming system and puts the family at risk. High value cash crops that are planted on all of the farmer's land are of little help to the poorest farmers averse to risking their multiple sources of sustenance for a single crop.

What can be done?

Supporting the family farm requires a hard look at the social systems and political policies that block a family's success. Once a development agency understands these forces, it is compelled to work with experts to advocate for change.

The development agency also must determine if appropriate government resources are available to assist the small farm. Many families do not have the time to seek out such resources or to advocate in favor of bringing them to their community.

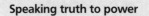

Speaking truth to power

In Cambodia, a microfinance program serves thousands of farm families. The development agency works closely with national policy makers to create regulations favorable to programs that would serve these families on a permanent basis. The new laws support the rights of the poor by providing a national legal structure that allows international PVOs and other institutions to provide regulated, permanent financial services to the poorest families. The new laws ensure the poor also have access to critical business support services for economic growth that benefits all.

Some cardinal rules

Advocacy is a skill. It requires research to identify laws, systems and policies harmful to the family farm. It also requires research to identify resources already available but not yet tapped. It requires knowledge of the farm family's priorities. It requires organization of dozens of different stakeholders – families; community organizations; local agricultural, credit, and educational organizations; as well as universities and research centers. It requires the ability to bring these groups and factors together to produce strategies that will effect the desired change.

Let the locals lead

Advocacy efforts can place local families at risk. If asked, farm families may reject placing their children, farm activities, animals and homes in peril for a cause they deem less important than their short-term well-being. Advocacy can stir reactions and even punishing consequences for the farm family if not sensitively orchestrated.

Development agencies involved in any level of advocacy must let local farm communities identify and prioritize the issues that they believe most urgent. The development agency must understand divisions within the community and must be willing to assist in every step of the advocacy effort. Advocacy needs to be a product of consensus and democratic decision making. Close collaboration with families will prevent unnecessary risk.

Advocacy in action

In Jharkhand, India, a local organization helped thousands of the poorest farming women develop savings and credit groups, called Self Help Groups. These groups of 20 women saved money each month and lent the savings to one another as needed. Once they had saved for six months, the local organization encouraged the groups to ask a nearby bank for more credit.

The bank lent them four times their savings, loans which they used for a variety of farming activities like raising chickens, building brick kilns or growing groundnuts. The bank lent to these women only because determined advocacy organizations lobbied the government earlier to create policies and new resources for local banks to lend to the poorest. These resources are now available throughout India helping 7 million families.

Start simply

Many development agencies with a focus on one specialty or type of program, like agricultural extension, believe that advocacy requires them to move into the arena of political lobbying. They become overwhelmed at the magnitude of the effort they believe is required, then feel paralyzed and fail to make simple, effective efforts.

This need not be the case. Going to the local government office and informing officials that several villages could use the services of a health center is advocacy. Going to the local bank and introducing bankers to potential farming clients is advocacy. Going to the middleman and asking him to meet with farmers to discuss market strategies is advocacy. Linking farm families to already available services is advocacy.

Partner with the pros

Many countries have strong lobbying entities already in place. These organizations have been specifically set up and staffed to undertake effective advocacy at various political levels. If a development agency makes use of these resources properly, it can expand the impact of its own work very quickly. Perhaps an advocacy organization is already working on an issue imperative to the health of farm communities in a given watershed. The community may need the support of the development agency to do background research or gather farm families for group interviews about the status quo.

Ally with others

Strength in numbers is essential for effective advocacy. Development agencies do well to support the work of the pros and to form alliances with similar organizations and build coalitions around key issues.

Think locally, act globally

Cross-border issues between nations can jeopardize the small family farm. For example, in Colombia farm families growing cocoa for chocolate have farms adjacent to farmers growing coca bushes for export cocaine. National and international initiatives to destroy coca bushes by

aerial herbicide-spraying leads to the destruction of all sprayed crops, not just coca. A more balanced approach might involve advocating in favor of measures in countries that purchase the cocaine to suppress the market for the crop.

Development agencies should understand the problems facing farm families, as well as the transnational or macro issues that contribute to those problems. Only by including the factors caused by globalization can the development agency design an appropriate strategy for advocacy.

Zimbabwe

Take home message

Work with pros

Link with organizations that make advocacy their main focus. Build coalitions with farm communities and other organizations to create strength in numbers.

Listen to the family

Ensure the chosen advocacy effort is the farm family's priority and not the priority of the development agency.[1]

---

[1] For sensitive or macro-level issues like debt relief, HIV/AIDS, extractive industries, child labor and fair trade, development agencies can advocate and lobby for change in cross-agency and cross-national coalitions without involving or putting the vulnerable populations they work with at risk.

Speaking truth to power

Advocacy in support of the family farm occurs at many levels. It can be as simple as a group of women farmers meeting with a town official to ask why the farm–market roadwork he promised before the election has never been completed. It can be as complicated as a cross-agency, cross-national initiative to reduce child labor through national legislation, local regulations and consumer education. Both types of advocacy are important.

CHAPTER 12

Breaking the rules: the family farm in crisis

Highlights

Emergencies and crises have a dramatic impact on the farm and NGO working context. Rules and guiding principles of sound development may need to be modified for emergencies. NGOs should seek creative, practical, flexible ways to support farm families in responding to and recovering from crisis.

The dilemma

A farm family in Uganda loses three of its members to AIDS. Two more are sick. The seventeen-year-old daughter, absent her parents, must care for her grandmother and look after her younger brothers and sisters. She is also left to manage the fields and animals.

In West Bengal, a farm is underwater for a full five days before the flooding recedes – the home of mud and thatch washed away, the livestock drowned, the rice paddies buried in mud and stones. Two teenage sons are ill with typhus.

A farm family in El Salvador finds its goat pen at the bottom of a newly formed ditch, the tin roof to their home lies next to the house, the kitchen floor is split in two. A collapsed wall pins the father to the ground. Just minutes ago, an earthquake struck.

A family in Cambodia steals away from its farm in the middle of the night. The next day, a rocket is aimed at the walls of their humble home. In seconds it crumbles. A few minutes later, stray bullets kill all livestock. The family returns four years later to rice fields overrun with weeds, fishponds dry and silt-filled and the sun-bleached bones

Labor of love

In rural Zimbabwe, where the rule was to earn a profit from farm activities, farm families would not hire people they feared had AIDS, as they might not be relied upon to show up for work regularly. Credit agencies refused to give them loans, lest they not be able to repay.

A local church sensitized the community to the harm caused by stigmatizing people with AIDS. When people agreed they all had to pull together, they created a community garden. The harvested produce was given only to AIDS and orphan-headed households. Any surplus was sold. Proceeds were used to buy medicines and pay school fees for AIDS-affected families.

of their water buffalo jutting from the ground.

What can be done?

Disease, floods, earthquakes, fire and war can obliterate a small, prosperous farm in weeks, days, seconds. This is the family farm in crisis. Its situation does not call for the patient practice of conservation farming. There is neither the time nor the available labor. The farm and the farming community require a jump-start, a chance to get back on their feet quickly. To help in times of natural and manmade disaster, the relief worker must often break the rules the development worker follows in stable times, rules like avoiding subsidies and giving gifts that foster dependency.

Where sustainable agriculture calls for new knowledge and the enduring patient labor of healthy families to turn raw land into a lively balance of dozens of farming activities, enriching and recycling natural resources, emergency agriculture calls for a completely different set of solutions. Sustainable agriculture projects in development programs ask families to create green manure by turning legumes into the soil or show how to improve the viability of saved seeds. Yet, emergency agriculture programs often provide seeds, plant cuttings, tools and chemical

The forgotten half

In Nicaragua, an international agency provided emergency relief to families whose lives were devastated by Hurricane Mitch. The agency gave seeds and tools to the families, which the men, who were in charge of the production side of the farm activities, used. The relief workers neglected to interview the women. These women needed grinding mills, cooking pots and buckets to carry water. Without cooking and processing tools, they had a difficult time feeding their families on the corn and beans the men produced.

fertilizers to the farm family to see them through at least one harvest.

In populations where 25% of the households are affected by HIV/AIDS, families may not have enough labor to apply basic organic farming methods, which tend to be labor-intensive. Children find themselves taking care of grandparents, looking after younger children and farming the fields at the same time. Many crises place labor in short supply and call for at least short-term, supplemental use of low-labor methods, like increasing chemical fertilizers, herbicide weed controls and pesticide insect controls that may not be environmentally sound in the long run.

In situations where refugees are forced to resettle onto land not their own, they may lack the tools to build shelter or the fuel to cook meals. In these cases, families may feel forced to mine the nearby forest for tent poles or cooking fuel. They may not have the means to repay loans, so credit is useless. The wise development agency will plan for this, and when the immediate crisis is resolved, they will offer short-term food aid and tree saplings to landowners robbed of their forests. They may also offer small grants instead of loans.

In situations where a whole community is in crisis, the development agency may find it inappropriate to focus on the poorest families when all families are in need and all need emergency relief to bring the community back to life.

Yet, even in times of emergency, some rules must never be broken. Talking to families and understanding their situations is paramount to providing good interventions.

Real building blocks?

After an earthquake rocked the rural areas of Northern India, a well-meaning development organization offered cash to villagers to help clear debris, dig fish ponds and reservoirs and construct animal fences. After some time, the organization returned with brick-making equipment so families could make bricks to rebuild their homes. The organization found two things:

1) villagers had become so used to receiving cash, they no longer had any interest in contributing their labor to the effort

2) women were performing most of the hard labor while men supervised.

Had the organization supplied building equipment to replace traditional assets and involved women from the beginning of the relief and reconstruction period, they may have had a better chance of getting community participation when it was needed.

Also, building on the investment people have already made before a crisis – in time, money, personal or physical effort – will yield activities that communities will sustain after a crisis period. Alas, after a crisis, programs often inject external finance in order to 'get' people involved in brand new activities, undermining family efforts to build

The family farm in crisis

Whether a volcano in Goma erupts and covers the family farm with lava, whether a five-day rain floods farms in West Bengal or whether armed conflict in the Sudan forces families to flee their farms, normal life is interrupted and farm assets are destroyed. After the immediate crisis passes, families need support to rebuild. But the support they need, as they make the transition back to normal life, can be very different from the development support they were provided before the emergency. Depending on the nature of the emergency, families may also find themselves slipping in and out of crisis as armed conflict resumes or as floods are replaced by drought. Supporting farm families under such conditions is challenging, requires flexibility and depends on constant learning.

on previous strengths to create something lasting and meaningful. What gets people involved is to support non-harmful coping mechanisms used during the crisis and to build on the traditional activities they engaged in before the crisis.

Noticing gender issues or the traditional roles and labor patterns of various household members will improve a relief effort, as will involving families in decision making.

Take home message

Break the rules wisely

In times of crisis, help families to jump-start their farms for productive activity. Include both women and men in post-emergency assistance. Be flexible, but sensible, in delivering aid.

Conclusions

The simple life. Or is it? We wrote *The Resilient Family Farm* partly to show that behind the seemingly uncomplicated life of the smallholder farm family lies a world teeming with challenges and activity, requiring clever solutions for complex, dynamic constraints.

But there is a second purpose to this book – sharing a portrait of the few families who are able to escape the fate of their neighbors – lives of poverty. These exceptional families manage something we are calling a resilient farm. They rear healthier children, raise sturdier animals, harvest more from their crops, manage to avert disease, withstand drought better and have more food and cash on hand than their neighbors across the hill with weaker children, fewer animals, sparser harvests and less income. Both families farm the same rocky soils, are subject to the same vagaries of weather, operate within the same economic constraints and uphold the same local customs, yet one family fares far better. What is their secret?

As we demonstrated in Part I, chances are good that the resilient farm family produces not only a diversity of goods, but recycles and renews resources and waste, rehabilitates the land, protects their water supply and maintains moderate tree cover. Their farm is continually reborn and replenished for continued harvests, while resisting modest shocks and stresses.

We hope readers will walk away with a few lasting impressions. Resilient farmers sow their futures in very difficult environments – degraded natural resources, unstable governments, unfavorable policy and inequitable socio-economic systems. Yet somehow they succeed where others fail.

Although they are more capable than their neighbors, in the long run the odds are against them. They need support from donors and development agencies to protect the gains they have made, and they need the voices of concerned, educated citizens in other countries to advocate on their behalf against inequitable global trends and systems.

Their life of toil, testing, persistence and talent holds many natural processes and human technologies in balance. Their judicious management can steady the extremes of seasons and economies. Their nurturing and development of a resilient farm reaps a measure of stability, as the farm is able to sustain the family in times of moderate social, political and natural crises. Above all, donor and development agencies wishing to strengthen the efforts of these families must do so wisely and with humility, with fruitful intention and vast stores of respect, and they must take the time to do their homework.

This raises the third purpose for this book, providing suggestions for supporting resilient farmers and their less resilient neighbors more effectively than we have in the past. This is the subject of Part II of *The Resilient Family Farm*.

Three words have become the clarion call of many development organizations whose intent is to help the poor – do no harm. But in fact, harm is done. Well-meaning organizations devote many resources to relief and development work, earnestly seeking to improve the lot of rural farm families. Yet the effect of this work is often the reverse.

We say, 'We know best'. But we do not understand the risk a small farmer must take to follow our advice. We say, 'We know best'. But we do not understand how the one silver bullet that we are promoting disrupts the subtle web of farm activities on which livelihoods and cultures depend. We say, 'We know best'. But we do not understand how often farm outcomes are controlled and affected more by pressures and events 'off the farm' than by the work we do 'on the farm'.

As experts, we can no longer say we know best. Too often, the price for our best has been too high for small farm families. Unwittingly, we have contributed to trends that helped farm families strip their land of good soil, deplete their water tables, develop products with no market and place a greater burden on women and children. We did this partly through misguided intentions, partly through good intentions that went astray and partly through overconfidence in simple, short-term solutions that were inappropriate for far-reaching, multifaceted problems in dynamic and rapidly degrading environments.

We now understand that the problems of the poor are complex, but we are not yet sure how best to work together to combine the expertise of different sectors and disciplines to improve lives and livelihoods. We now understand the critical role of national and international forces in creating and maintaining problems of poverty and injustice, but we are not yet sure how to advocate for change, which issues to focus on and which audiences and decision makers to address. Although we have had some solid success helping smallholder farmers increase production in environmentally sound ways, we struggle to provide financial services that meet rural needs. We have also neglected marketing and income generation.

Part II of *The Resilient Family Farm* is a call for humility. It is a call for critical analysis and a new willingness to treat the problems of the rural poor as complex and worthy of our best creative thinking. To support improved quality of development programs, we have provided readers with many guiding principles. They go beyond the lessons of past successes and failures, seeking ways to break out of familiar, but counterproductive patterns.

We ask experts to draw on equal measures of respect, collaboration, good listening and an appreciation of local wisdom as they apply their expert solutions. As we begin to probe the complexities and links within the world of smallholder farm families, and as we begin to analyze the links and relationships between the world of rural families and the larger world, we can also begin to focus on root causes, not just symptoms of problems. This will enable us to serve as more effective catalysts for positive, profound change.

As holistic, farm-savvy and income-conscious approaches are firmly adopted, we are confident development organizations will look forward to strengthening rural farm life, adding the good practices of the natural sciences, engineering, economics, public health, sociology and education. Tempered by humility and a willingness to listen and learn, professionals from these scientific and social disciplines will become real experts, truly useful to the farm and farm family. Used wisely, we believe their expertise will help smallholder farms become truly resilient family farms.

Glossary

Acre: a unit of land equal to 0.405 hectares; 4,050 square meters or 43,560 square feet.

Agriculture: the art and science of farming. Activities include cultivating the soil, managing water, producing crops and raising livestock.

Agricultural extension: dissemination of improved technologies through training and field visits to farm communities.

Agro-ecology: the combined sciences of agriculture and ecology. Agro-ecosystems are those ecosystems that are modified by humans for the purpose of agricultural production of food, fuel, clothing, medicine, bedding, animal species, etc. Agro-ecosystems involve complementary components, using different soil depths for different plants, different types and timing of labor for different purposes, different amounts of light for light- or shade-loving plants. Agro-ecosystems also involve synergy, as one element improves conditions for other elements – crops that repel weeds, insects or disease for a companion crop; plants that produce nutrients that another plant needs; crops that cover and protect the soil for a companion crop or a later crop, etc.

Agro-forestry: growing trees on the same land as crops and livestock.

Agronomist: a professional trained in the agricultural sciences.

Alley cropping: a crop management method of planting several rows of trees between rows of crops.

Annual: in agriculture, an annual crop refers to a crop that grows, reaches maturity and is harvested within one year or one growing season.

Aquaculture: growing fish (or plants) in water as a productive endeavor.

Aquifer: a geological formation beneath the soil that holds and carries large amounts of sub-surface water through permeable rocks, gravel or sand.

Arid: climates with an average annual rainfall of less than 200 mm (about 8 inches).

Asset: tangible property with some value.

Bi-modal rainfall: when the annual rainy season is characterized by two distinct periods of rainfall separated by a dry spell.

Botanist: a specialist in the study of plants.

Bund: a dike or ridge of soil located on the contour of a slope to reduce erosion. Bunds are also used as a border around fields of water-flooded crops like paddy rice.

Commodity: a class of goods where individual products are undifferentiated in the eyes of the customer and therefore vulnerable to substitution. Competitors selling commodities find that customers often purchase them based soley on price. In agriculture, commodities refer to major grain and legume crops, as well as livestock.

Compost: a farm-made fertilizer consisting of decomposed organic matter (weeds, leaves, straw and other crop residue), kitchen scraps, ashes, manure and sometimes lime, urea fertilizer, chalk or rock phosphate. The final product of composting is rich, dark, crumbly 'humus'. (Because it is a labor-intensive fertilizer, compost is more appropriate for small spaces like kitchen gardens or high-value crops like market vegetable gardens. For large crop fields of maize, millet, rice or wheat, less labor-intensive soil amendments like green manure or bagged fertilizer are more appropriate. See also 'green manure'.)

Contour: an imaginary line on a slope that connects all points at the same elevation. A contour line is always perpendicular to the slope. Planting crops and placing bunds and infiltration ditches on the contour reduces soil and water erosion and usually increases yields.

Cover crop: an annual crop that is planted to protect the soil from evaporation, erosion and weed growth. Cover crops are also used to improve soil fertility and increase soil organic matter.

Crop: annual or perennial plants cultivated to yield products for humans and livestock. Crop products include grains, vegetables, fuel, fodder, clothing, fruit and flowers.

Depreciate: the loss in value of an asset over time.

Desertification: the process of decline in production due to land degradation and changing weather patterns in arid or semi-arid regions. Land can become so degraded, infertile or saline, that the process of desertification becomes irreversible.

Diversity (in agro-ecosystems): the quantity of different species, organisms and crops per unit area.

Ecology: the science of the relationship between organisms and their natural environments. Ecologically-sound, or environmentally-sound, agriculture refers to production activities that incorporate conservation or rehabilitation of natural resources, maintaining or improving the quality and quantity of soil, water and vegetation. Resources are recycled, losses are minimized and pollution is avoided or mitigated. Wherever possible, renewable resources are used in production.

Entomologist: an expert in insects.

Environmentally sound production: (see Ecology)

Extension: disseminating and sharing improved production methods and appropriate innovations through providing advice and training for farmers. Extensionists work with farmers to help solve local production problems, improve decision making and enhance farm management.

Fallow: when land is not cultivated for one or more growing seasons and is left to rest. Natural vegetation returns and is sometimes grazed.

Fertilizer: chemical or biochemical compounds that contain nutrients needed by plants. Compost and bedding manure are examples of 'natural' fertilizers that provide soil nutrients and improve a wide range of soil properties like soil structure, nutrient- and water-holding capacity, aeration, drainage and soil organic matter. Industrially-manufactured fertilizers are fast-acting, short-term suppliers of nutrients and need to be applied several times during the growing season. They do not provide many of the benefits of compost or green manure, and if overused, will harm beneficial soil life and contribute to degradation of soil texture. But commercial fertilizer requires less labor on the part of the farm family. Smallholder farmers tend to use a combination of the two kinds of fertilizer, when they can afford to buy commercial fertilizer.

Financial services: services that banks, microfinance organizations and other financial institutions offer their customers. Larger institutions provide a variety of services, but most offer simple loans and some sort of savings scheme.

Grading: sorting of products and produce based on certain characteristics.

Gray water: discarded household water from cleaning or bathing.

Green manure: any crop plant, but generally a nitrogen-fixing plant, that is grown and worked back into the soil as a natural fertilizer. Green manure can be used as a low-labor alternative to composting for fertilizing large cropping areas. See also 'compost'.

Green Revolution: a period of time in the 1960s and 1970s when agricultural productivity (production per unit area) increased dramatically through the use of high-yielding varieties and management for maximum yield.

Groundwater: sub-surface water that supplies wells and springs.

Guarantees: forms of security to ensure a lender is repaid. Guarantees can be financial or social.

Hardpan: a layer of compacted soil that resists penetration by roots and water.

Hectare: a unit of land that is equal to 2.47 acres or 10,000 square meters.

Horticulture: the science of gardening (vegetables, flowers, fruit).

Humus: the sweet smelling, rich, dark fertilizer produced through natural decomposition of forest litter, for example, or by composting. When added to soil, humus improves soil fertility, nutrient and water retention, drainage and aeration.

Hybrid seed: seed that is produced by crossing different varieties or species. When hybrid seed is planted with recommended fertilizer amounts, yields can be much greater than non-hybrids. However, yields cannot be maintained from saved seed in successive years, so hybrid seed must be purchased each year. Hybrids often lose the original disease- or drought-resistant traits of their parent lines, as the breeding process selects for traits that increase yield capacity. A judicious combination of 'traditional' varieties for some crops and, when cash is available, 'improved' hybrids for others is a common survival strategy of smallholder families.

Inputs: used here to refer to farm inputs like water, nutrients, solar energy, information, fertilizer, pesticides, herbicides, tools and processing equipment.

Legume, leguminous: any plant, shrub or tree in the Leguminosae family. With the help of soil bacteria belonging to the genus *Rhizobium*, leguminous plants have the ability to convert atmospheric nitrogen into a form of nitrogen in the soil that can be used by plants. Examples of legumes are beans, peas, alfalfas and trees in the *Acacia* and *Leucaena* genera.

Maize: another word for corn. Maize generally refers to the hardier field corn varieties, not sweet corn.

Manure: animal waste and stable litter of farm animals. This natural fertilizer is one of the oldest and, when managed and handled properly, one of the most effective fertilizers available to farmers.

Marketing: any activities related to bringing products to customers for the purpose of selling. Marketing activities include market research, product positioning, sales, product grading, pricing, processing, packaging, transporting and distributing.

Meteorologist: an expert in weather and weather forecasting.

Microenterprise: small business activities.

Microfinance: savings, credit and other financial services for low income and very poor people.

Micro-livestock: in this book, micro-livestock refers to smaller farmyard animals like goats, sheep, rabbits or poultry, rather than pigs or cows.

Monocropping: one crop per field. This is a management technique used in modern agriculture. Traditional agriculture often sows a mix of two or more crops in the same field, for example maize and beans in Central America or millet and cowpea in the Sahel.

Mulch: a layer of dead leaves, stalks or other plant matter, bark, stones or plastic that is spread on the surface of the soil between plants or rows to prevent evaporation from the soil, control weeds or regulate soil temperature.

NGO: Non-governmental organization. In this book NGO is used to refer to local organizations, as opposed to PVO, which is used to refer to international relief and development organizations.

Nitrogen-fixing plants: also referred to as leguminous, these plants take nitrogen from the air and, with the help of bacteria in the soil, transform it into a plant-available form that the leguminous plant itself and any surrounding plants can use.

Outputs: used here to refer to farm products or functions that result from farm activities. Outputs are consumed on the farm (grains, vegetables, fuelwood, livestock), reinvested on the farm (cover crops, manure), exchanged or sold.

Partners: Catholic Relief Services works through local non-governmental organizations called 'partners' to implement development projects. Working through partners improves local capacity building, long-term continuity of activities and ensures benefits that continue after project funding ends. Many CRS partners are part of a broad network of Catholic agencies and parishes around the world, and many are local secular development organizations.

Perennial: A crop or plant that has a lifespan of more than two years. Trees are 'perennials'. (Bean or wheat crops are 'annuals'.)

Positive deviant: A person whose exceptional behavior, practices or innovations make him/her more successful than others in the same group.

PTA: Parent Teacher Association. PTA is used here to refer to any community-based organization that supports a local school.

PVO: Private Voluntary Organization. An international relief and development organization such as Oxfam, CARE and World Vision. PVO is used here to distinguish international non-governmental organizations from national NGOs.

Resilient farm: A farm that balances production, conservation and income generation; one that balances the use and replenishment of natural resources; has diverse animal, tree and crop production systems; recycles and uses resources efficiently. Resilient farms can provide modestly for a smallholder family's food and economic security, while withstanding moderately severe fluctuations and crises.

Residue: this refers to the non-harvested or residual portion of a crop – leaves, straw, stalks, branches, stems, husks, etc.

Retail: the sale of goods and services to consumers (see wholesale).

Rotation: a cropping cycle in which different crops are planted in succession each year to revitalize and protect the soil. Sometimes the rotation includes a fallow year.

Seed banks: Seeds stored in a silo, usually by a group of farm families for later sale, consumption and planting.

Self-help groups: groups of women who save small amounts of money each month, lend savings to one another in the form of small loans and when ready, borrow additional money from the bank.

Semi-arid: climates where annual precipitation ranges from about 200–900 mm (8–35 inches) and where timing of rainfall may vary widely, making cropped, rainfed agriculture a challenge.

Smallholder: this term generally refers to farm families that survive by agricultural production on small landholdings, 5 hectares or less – generally much less.

Solidarity groups: groups of women, organized by an NGO, in which members agree to approve and guarantee one another's loans extended to each by the NGO. (CRS microfinance programs generally work with women clients.)

Subsidy: funds in the form of cash, in-kind payments and tax relief from public and humanitarian sources designated for the purpose of public good. Subsidies are important when the commercial sector cannot address social needs (schools, bridges) for lack of potential profit. Subsidies may cause harm if recipients become dependent on them or if they stifle economic and social initiative.

Subsistence agriculture: farming in which most of the production is geared toward feeding the farm family. Very little smallholder production today is completely subsistence-oriented, as every family needs some cash for school fees, shoes, medicine, tools, fertilizer, etc.

Sustainable agriculture: environmentally-sound farm production that conserves and protects natural resources for further production.

Tenure: right to property, through legal rights or custom. Tenure may include rights to land, water or trees.

Value-added processing: When the raw goods produced on a farm gain increased value because they have been roasted, peeled, graded, husked, ground, milled, dried, salted, pickled, baked or modified in some way to meet the needs or standards of customers.

Vetiver grass *(Vetiveria zizanoides)*: a coarse grass often planted in a row along the contour of slopes, growing quickly to form a very dense hedge that blocks passage of soil, slows rainfall runoff and helps spread rain evenly across the slope, so it soaks in where it falls. Established vetiver plantings are so effective that they can prevent mudslides in high intensity storms. (Board on Science and Technology for International Development. 1993. *Vetiver grass: A thin green line against erosion.* Washington, DC: National Academy Press.)

Village banks: similar to large solidarity groups, often with 20 to 50 women who meet regularly, review loan requests and guarantee that as a group, they will pay back the loans of all its members to the NGO who provided the initial loan. Most village banks require that members save regularly.

Water harvesting: collecting or storing rainfall or surface water from a river or stream in barrels, 'tanks' or micro-reservoirs in the soil to provide water for domestic use, crops or livestock.

Waterlogging: when a soil becomes saturated with water. Water replaces most of the aeration pores and drainage paths in the soil and can kill crops when the saturation persists.

Watershed: an area of land bordered by high elevation points in which all the water falling within those borders drains to the same river or body of water.

Wholesale: the sale of goods and services to businesses which distribute them (often after adding value) to other wholesalers, retailers or consumers.

Resources

Bornstein, David. 1999. *The Price of a Dream: The Story of the Grameen Bank and the Idea that is Helping the Poor to Change Their Lives.* (Chicago, Illinois, USA: The University of Chicago Press)

Bunch, Roland. 1985. *Two Ears of Corn: A Guide to People-Centered Agricultural Improvement.* (Oklahoma City, Oklahoma, USA: World Neighbors, 5116 N. Portland Ave, Oklahoma City)

Burgess, Ann; Grace Maina; Philip Harris and Stephanie Harris. 1998. *How to Grow a Balanced Diet: A Handbook for Community Workers.* (London, UK: VSO Books)

Ledgerwood, Joanna; Ian Johnson and Jean-Michel Severino. 2001. *Microfinance Handbook: An Institutional and Financial Perspective.* (Washington, DC: The World Bank)

Reijntjes, Coen; Bertus Haverkort and Ann Waters-Bayer. 1992. *Farming for the Future: An Introduction to Low-External-Input and Sustainable Agriculture.* (Oxford, UK: Macmillan Press)

Rutherford, Stuart. 2001. *The Poor and Their Money.* (Delhi, India: Oxford University Press)

Whiteside, Martin. 1998. *Living Farms: Encouraging Sustainable Smallholder Agriculture in Southern Africa.* (London, UK: Earthscan Publications Ltd)

Wilson, Kim. 2001. *Principled Practices in Microfinance.* (Baltimore, Maryland, USA: Catholic Relief Services, 209 W. Fayette)

Ecuador

About CRS and CRS Agriculture

Catholic Relief Services was founded in 1943 to assist the poor living outside the USA. CRS works to alleviate suffering, and to promote human development, peace and justice. CRS has programs in agriculture, education, health, HIV/AIDS, microfinance, peacebuilding and water/sanitation in over 80 countries, serving the poor solely on the basis of need, not creed, race or nationality.

CRS agriculture programs seek to improve family well-being through rural economic development and environmental stewardship. Program activities are based on assessing local needs and opportunities. They include crop and horticultural production, rural credit, recovery from disaster, soil and water conservation, agro-forestry, livestock production, integrated pest management, land tenure, processing and marketing.

CRS partner agencies and agriculture projects work with the poorest farm families and communities, with farm laborers, the landless, rural communities with high rates of HIV/AIDS and victims of man-made and natural disasters. CRS works with farmers as partners and treats farming as a family-run business, acknowledging that rural communities are linked to markets and that farm families need income for off-farm products and services. CRS agriculture programs focus on farming systems, supporting diverse production for risk reduction and food security, while linking production to conservation. Finally, CRS uses watershed approaches, fostering cross-community collaboration for resource protection and upstream/downstream cooperation to meet competing needs.

About CRS Microfinance

CRS invests in rural economies around the world by sponsoring a network of local partner organizations that offer credit and savings services (microfinance) to very poor farm families, helping them to make timely investments in farm activities, small businesses, their homes and children. CRS continuously seeks to support innovations that best serve the financial needs of the farm family.

Increasingly we are including more effective ways to match savings and loan products to the seasons and cycles of rural life. We focus on women clients, link loans to savings and begin with small amounts, so clients learn to manage debt as they accumulate new wealth. Farm families benefit from good credit and savings services as they reduce dependence on exploitative moneylenders and keep savings out of the hands of needy friends and relatives. Through regular savings, families build cash reserves to cushion emergencies and use both loans and savings to make important investments in education, farm and home.

About the authors

Gaye Burpee is Senior Technical Adviser for Natural Risk Management and Agriculture/Environment in South Asia. She was previously Director of the Technical Services Unit, Program Quality and Support Department at Catholic Relief Services (CRS), and Senior Technical Adviser for Agriculture/ Environment. Prior to joining CRS, she was a soil scientist for the Central American Hillsides Project (CIAT, International Center for Tropical Agriculture), developing simple, farmer-friendly tools for monitoring change in soil quality in collaboration with Honduran farmers. Dr Burpee specialized in soil physics and sustainable agriculture in graduate studies at Michigan State University, teaching soil physics and graduate courses in plant science teaching methods for diverse students. She conducted research on sustainable alternatives for potato production in temperate zones, as well as crop production and vegetative cover for harsh tropical environments, served as Director of an economic household survey of Grenada, West Indies, and as a Research Associate at University of Michigan's Institute for Social Research, focusing on socio-economic and political survey research. She completed Peace Corps service in Grenada and St Vincent, West Indies.

Kim Wilson is Deputy Regional Director for Program Quality in South Asia, Catholic Relief Services. She was previously a Senior Technical Adviser for Microfinance and Director of the CRS Microfinance Unit. Prior to joining CRS, she was Deputy Director of Working Capital, the largest microfinance organization in the USA and recipient of the Presidential Award for Excellence in 1997. Ms Wilson has consulted for UNDP (United Nations Development Programme), USAID (United States Agency for International Development) and several US-based PVOs (private voluntary organizations). Prior to her work in microfinance, Ms Wilson was a partner in a Boston-based venture capital firm, as well as adjunct professor at Boston University's Graduate School of Management. She is a guest lecturer at Harvard University's Graduate School of Design and teaches in the Microenterprise Development Institute of Southern New Hampshire University. She has published in *Journal of Microfinance* and *Microbanking Bulletin*.

Index

building infrastructure 101–8
business development service
109–19
  market chains 61–2
  participatory methods 85
  problem of 28–9
  production–marketing chain
  124–5
  support for farm families 73–87
diet 19–20, 22–3, 54
disasters 149–53
diseases 39–41, 65
diversity 50–1, 52
  enterprises 116–17
  products 122–3
  reducing risk 46–8
Dominican Republic 116

ecological systems 81–3
economic systems 57–69, 81–3
Ecuador 58, 106, 142
education 24, 25–6, 53
efficiency 64–5, 66–8
Egypt 62
emergencies 53, 149–53
entrepreneurs 18
environment 31–41, 74
Ethiopia 105
ethnicity 26
extension *see* agricultural extension
  services

farm assets, building 101–7
farm enterprises 109–19
farm families
  agricultural system 43–55
  economic systems 57–69
  labor 77–9
  natural environment 31–41
  roles 15–18
  social environment 15–30
  support for 73–87
farmer scientists 16, 17, 96–7
farming systems 91–2
fertilizers 35–7
financing
  coordination of interventions 84

Core Triangle 62–3
  farm enterprises 111
  financial services 129–38
fire 37–9
fish ponds 3, 4–5, 8–9, 47, 66–8
food 19–20, 22–3, 54
forest 130–2

Gambia 50
garlic 3, 39
gender 24–5
  emergency help 150, 151, 153
  Green Revolution 50, 77–8
globalization of markets 28
government policies 18
  advocacy 141–7
  financing programs 62
  risks 46
  threats to economic systems 65
grassroots associations 137
Green Revolution 50, 73–7, 92
group activities 117
growth 109–19
Guatemala 35, 97, 102

Haiti 91
health 22–3
  coordination of interventions 84
  investment in 62
  training 54
high-return conservation farm 5
HIV/AIDS 49, 78, 150, 151
Honduras 48, 53, 92
honey 16, 28
humus 36, 37
hunger season 19
Hurricane Mitch 53, 150

income generation 109–19
  balance with conservation 77–8
  Core Triangle 59–63
India
  advocacy 144
  development programs 16, 25,
  46, 90
  earthquake help 151
  Green Revolution 76